Colonial Latin American Literature:
A Very Short Introduction

VERY SHORT INTRODUCTIONS are for anyone wanting a stimulating and accessible way in to a new subject. They are written by experts, and have been published in more than 25 languages worldwide.

The series began in 1995, and now represents a wide variety of topics in history, philosophy, religion, science, and the humanities. The VSI library now contains 300 volumes—a Very Short Introduction to everything from ancient Egypt and Indian philosophy to conceptual art and cosmology—and will continue to grow in a variety of disciplines.

Very Short Introductions available now:

ADVERTISING Winston Fletcher
AFRICAN HISTORY
    John Parker and Richard Rathbone
AGNOSTICISM Robin Le Poidevin
AMERICAN IMMIGRATION
    David A. Gerber
AMERICAN POLITICAL PARTIES
    AND ELECTIONS L. Sandy Maisel
THE AMERICAN PRESIDENCY
    Charles O. Jones
ANARCHISM Colin Ward
ANCIENT EGYPT Ian Shaw
ANCIENT GREECE Paul Cartledge
ANCIENT PHILOSOPHY Julia Annas
ANCIENT WARFARE
    Harry Sidebottom
ANGELS David Albert Jones
ANGLICANISM Mark Chapman
THE ANGLO-SAXON AGE John Blair
THE ANIMAL KINGDOM
    Peter Holland
ANIMAL RIGHTS David DeGrazia
ANTISEMITISM Steven Beller
THE APOCRYPHAL GOSPELS
    Paul Foster
ARCHAEOLOGY Paul Bahn
ARCHITECTURE Andrew Ballantyne
ARISTOCRACY William Doyle
ARISTOTLE Jonathan Barnes
ART HISTORY Dana Arnold
ART THEORY Cynthia Freeland
ATHEISM Julian Baggini
AUGUSTINE Henry Chadwick

AUTISM Uta Frith
BARTHES Jonathan Culler
BEAUTY Roger Scruton
BESTSELLERS John Sutherland
THE BIBLE John Riches
BIBLICAL ARCHAEOLOGY Eric H. Cline
BIOGRAPHY Hermione Lee
THE BLUES Elijah Wald
THE BOOK OF MORMON
    Terryl Givens
THE BRAIN Michael O'Shea
BRITISH POLITICS Anthony Wright
BUDDHA Michael Carrithers
BUDDHISM Damien Keown
BUDDHIST ETHICS Damien Keown
CANCER Nicholas James
CAPITALISM James Fulcher
CATHOLICISM Gerald O'Collins
THE CELL
    Terence Allen and Graham Cowling
THE CELTS Barry Cunliffe
CHAOS Leonard Smith
CHILDREN'S LITERATURE
    Kimberley Reynolds
CHOICE THEORY Michael Allingham
CHRISTIAN ART Beth Williamson
CHRISTIAN ETHICS D. Stephen Long
CHRISTIANITY Linda Woodhead
CITIZENSHIP Richard Bellamy
CLASSICAL MYTHOLOGY
    Helen Morales
CLASSICS
    Mary Beard and John Henderson

Available soon:

For more information visit our web site
www.oup.co.uk/general/vsi/

Rolena Adorno

COLONIAL LATIN AMERICAN LITERATURE

A Very Short Introduction

OXFORD
UNIVERSITY PRESS

OXFORD
UNIVERSITY PRESS

Oxford University Press, Inc., publishes works that further
Oxford University's objective of excellence
in research, scholarship, and education.

Oxford   New York
Auckland   Cape Town   Dar es Salaam   Hong Kong   Karachi
Kuala Lumpur   Madrid   Melbourne   Mexico City   Nairobi
New Delhi   Shanghai   Taipei   Toronto

With offices in
Argentina   Austria   Brazil   Chile   Czech Republic   France   Greece
Guatemala   Hungary   Italy   Japan   Poland   Portugal   Singapore
South Korea   Switzerland   Thailand   Turkey   Ukraine   Vietnam

Copyright © 2011 by Oxford University Press, Inc.

Published by Oxford University Press, Inc.
198 Madison Avenue, New York, NY 10016

www.oup.com

Library of Congress Cataloging-in-Publication Data
Adorno, Rolena.
Colonial Latin American literature: a very short introduction / Rolena Adorno.
p. cm.—(Very short introductions)
Includes bibliographical references and index.
ISBN 978-0-19-975502-8 (pbk.)
1. Spanish American literature—To 1800—History and criticism.
2. Latin America—In literature.
3. Imperialism in literature.
4. Latin America—Discovery and exploration—Spanish.
5. Indians—First contact with Europeans.
6. Spanish language—Latin America—History.   I. Title.
PQ7081.A36 2011
860.9'98—dc22
2011007317

5 7 9 8 6

Printed in Great Britain
by Ashford Colour Press Ltd., Gosport, Hants.
on acid-free paper

To my girls, for then, now, and always.

Acknowledgments

My pursuit of the colonial Latin American literary record would be impossible without the Beinecke Rare Book and Manuscript Library at Yale and the John Carter Brown Library at Brown University, whose collections are always put cheerfully at my disposal by curators who understand the preciousness of old books and appreciate the scholarly greed with which their patrons devour them. For this project, Karen Nangle at the Beinecke and Leslie Tobias-Olsen at the JCB deserve special mention. As always, Ivan Boserup at the Royal Library in Copenhagen has provided quick and cordial assistance. My graduate students at Yale, Ricardo Monsalve C. and Elena Pellús Pérez, and my research assistant, Yale senior Joseph Bolognese, deserve recognition for their unfailing intellectual, technical, and moral support. They make scholarship worthwhile. My distinguished colleague and friend Roberto González Echevarría merits my deep appreciation for a decades-long intellectual companionship that makes the journey ever new.

Contents

List of illustrations

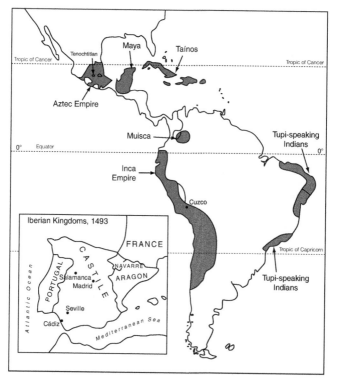

1. Major Amerindian cultures and Iberian kingdoms in the fifteenth century

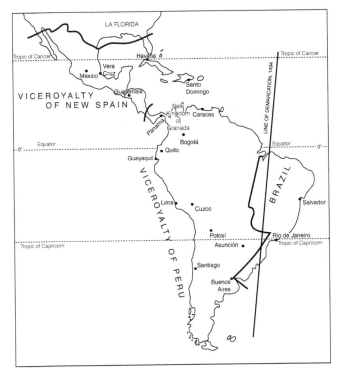

2. The viceroyalties of New Spain and Peru in the sixteenth and seventeenth centuries

Introduction

The emergence of the Americas on the world stage is a story first announced in Spanish, and that story defines colonial Latin American literature. Interpreting the nature and meaning of lands and peoples unknown to Europe, how they fit into the world as defined by the West, and how they should or did relate to it occupied able minds from Columbus's announcement in 1493 of his first successful transatlantic voyage through the era of Latin American independence. Courtly humanist scholars, tonsured friars, conquistador captains, ordinary foot soldiers, colonial functionaries from Spain, indigenous Americans for whom Spanish was not a first language, learned nuns, exiled Jesuits, and erudite promoters of political and cultural independence created this heterogeneous literary tradition.

"Colonial Latin American literature" is a useful misnomer. "Colonial" has a clear temporal referent: the more than three centuries of Spanish domination in the Americas, from Columbus's first landing in 1492 to the independence of Spanish-held territories, excepting Cuba, Puerto Rico, and the Philippines, achieved from 1809 through the 1820s. "Latin America" is a name that appeared after independence, and its referent is spatial, cultural, and linguistically historical, alluding to the common origin of the Romance vernaculars, the language of imperial Rome. Anticipated by Ranke, Hegel, and Tocqueville, the concept

"Latin America" was formulated by a young French intellectual, Michel Chevalier, and the explicit term was coined by South Americans living abroad in exile.

In 1875 the Colombian writer José María Torres Caicedo remarked that since 1851 he and other members of the exiled Spanish American community in Europe referred to Spanish-speaking America, including the Caribbean, as "Latin America." They did so, he wrote, not in disavowal of the Spanish language and its cultural heritage but rather in recognition of the new term's broader purchase, with Spain's former American colonies being members but not the sole inhabitants of a larger cultural domain that included the Portuguese and the French (this, in contradistinction to the British, Dutch, Danish, and other interests in the Americas).

Inasmuch as the colonial writings of the Spanish-speaking Americas were first gathered together as the origins of the respective national literatures during the nineteenth-century post-independence period, I likewise place this colonial-era literary production under the rubric of the more inclusive concept: "Latin America" transcends the language in which the works ultimately have come down to us (some were conceived and first written in indigenous Amerindian languages) and signals the broader, diverse cultural complex to which all these writings pertain without pretending to be its exclusive proprietors.

Finally, "literature": Many of the writers examined here narrated and debated historical events, others scrutinized the world of nature, and still others gave epic or lyric expression to the same phenomena, exercising their literary imaginations and leaning on the assemblage of Western literary reference and allusion to give voice to what was essentially or uniquely American. Constituted by a wide-ranging assortment of insights and interpretations, the field is seen here not as a collection of serial, unrelated items but as more systematic, held together by the glue of authors' references to America, to one another, and to other common reference points.

When many of these authors were writing, the eighteenth-century concept of literature had not yet emerged, but they were keenly aware of the differences between imaginative fictional writings, such as the romances of chivalry, against which the earliest of them contrasted their "true histories." They appreciated the mandate to write truthfully about historical matters and celebrated the prerogatives of epic and lyric poetry. The colonial writers' capacity for observation, interpretation, synthesis, and engaging expression about a world unknown and unseen by Europe are the qualities that make colonial writings worth reading, and it is what makes them literary.

The study of colonial Latin American literature began during the early post-independence period when poets, essayists, and critics collected and published the works of their predecessors and peers. They took a Pan-American approach, as did such great polymaths as the Venezuelan Andrés Bello, beginning in the 1820s, and the Argentine Juan María Gutiérrez, from the 1840s on. Bridging Enlightenment learning and Romantic aspirations for poetic and political self-expression, they and their successors studied and anthologized colonial-era poetry and prose.

Some of the monuments of the prose tradition, such as the chronicles of discovery and conquest, had already been canonized in their eighteenth-century publication in Madrid by Andrés González de Barcia, a member of the Royal Council of Castile and one of the founders of the Spanish Royal Academy. Although Barcia's goal had been to celebrate the past glories of Spain against its international detractors, an ironically unintended consequence of his work a century later was to provide the emerging Latin American republics with modern editions of some of the writings on which they would ground their emergent literatures.

Study of colonial-era literary production continued apace from the mid-nineteenth century into the twentieth, especially in the Americas, but also in Spain, France, England, and Germany. In the United States in the 1940s and 1950s prominent Latin American intellectuals teaching in U.S. universities explained Latin America to their Anglo-American audiences by starting with Columbus. Notable in this regard are the works that foregrounded Spanish colonial literary and intellectual history, such as the Chilean Arturo Torres Ríoseco's *The Epic of Latin American Literature* (1942), the Venezuelan Mariano Picón-Salas's *A Cultural History of Spanish America: From Conquest to Independence* (1944), the Dominican Pedro Henríquez Ureña's *Literary Currents in Hispanic America* (1945, which he had presented in 1940–41 as Harvard University's prestigious Charles Eliot Norton Lectures), and the Argentine Enrique Anderson Imbert's *Spanish American Literature: A History* (1954).

Their North American peers were few but influential. Irving A. Leonard's *Books of the Brave* and Lewis Hanke's *The Spanish Struggle for Justice in the Conquest of America* both appeared in 1949 and have been in print ever since. Exploring, respectively, Spain's book trade with the Americas and studying Spain's intellectual engagement with the moral issues of imposing rule on conquered peoples, Leonard and Hanke followed a path that Thomas Jefferson had charted when in 1787 he wrote that "the ancient part of American history is written chiefly in Spanish."

Leonard was central to the development of English-language Spanish colonial literary studies in the United States. Alongside his pathbreaking work of the 1920s through 1940s on the transatlantic book trade, he became a major scholar of the Hispanic Baroque, called "el Barroco de Indias" ("the Baroque of the Indies") by Picón-Salas, whose cultural history Leonard translated into English in 1962. Spanning three decades, Leonard's work, from his biography in 1929 of the great Mexican creole Baroque writer and scientist Carlos de Sigüenza y Góngora, to his panoramic *Baroque Times in Old Mexico* of 1959, set the stage for generations of subsequent study of the Spanish American Baroque.

Also in 1959 Miguel León-Portilla charted an entirely new course for colonial writings by publishing Spanish translations of Nahuatl accounts of the conquest of Mexico. León-Portilla's anthology, titled the "Vision of the Vanquished" (*Visión de los vencidos*), appeared in English in 1962 as *The Broken Spears: The Aztec Account of the Conquest of Mexico*. Thus native Amerindian accounts of conquest, custom, belief, and ritual were collected in early colonial times (there are virtually no surviving strictly pre-Columbian sources), and have taken their rightful place as part of the Latin American literary and cultural heritage.

A significant catalyst to the launch of colonial literary studies came in the 1960s with the novelists of the Latin American Boom, that is, the burst of first-rate novels accompanied by their translations and the internationalization of their readership. Their forerunner was the Cuban novelist Alejo Carpentier, who read the accounts of Spanish discovery and conquest, brought them to life in the crucible of his fiction, and provided the literary epoch-defining insight that the seemingly marvelous in the New World was, actually, real (*lo real maravilloso*). The "Boom" writers, including Gabriel García Márquez, Mario Vargas Llosa, and Carlos Fuentes, and their successors, José Juan Saer, Abel Posse, and others, subsequently evoked the resonances of Latin America's origins in ways that have captivated readers ever since.

In the U.S. academy, the proliferation in the 1960s of area studies programs and, in the 1970s, women's studies and ethnic studies programs, broadened interests in the humanities to include works and traditions not previously canonized. From that period emerged new critical trends, including cultural studies, subaltern studies, and postcolonial studies, feminism and postfeminism, and gender and sexuality studies, all of which have found

Spanish-language colonial-era texts ripe for investigation. The 1992 Columbian Quincentenary cast a bright, sometimes blinding, spotlight on the field, and the early-twenty-first century bicentennial commemorations of the independence of the Latin American republics also reach back to the colonial heritage, focusing on texts and traditions seen as the origins of the respective national literatures.

Persuasion is at the heart of all the works that fill this colonial library. I have given a shape to these three centuries of colonial Latin American literature that I call "the polemics of possession." The bellicose meaning of "polemics" goes back to the ancient Greeks, and its later, sixteenth- through eighteenth-century disputational resonances are pertinent. In political history, "possession" has a legal meaning, as a concept of law. In natural history, possession refers to biological traits ranging from the recognizable and familiar to the seemingly marvelous. From the colonial-era writer's perspective, possession implies his or her own authority, be it political, broadly cultural, or strictly literary. The act of taking possession of authority is constitutive, not merely reflective, of social practices; it is a fundamental characteristic of colonial Latin American literature.

In some four overlapping incarnations these "polemics of possession" are the sixteenth-century debates about the political possession of the Indies, its lands, peoples, and resources; the seventeenth-century creole and Amerindian-heritage writers' literary efforts to take cultural possession of letters and learning, including the study of the pre-Columbian American past; the late eighteenth- and nineteenth-centuries' efforts to further the goals of cultural possession and take possession of political sovereignty in Latin America; and finally the nineteenth-century Latin American debates over how to take American possession of the Spanish language itself.

Persuasion is complemented by freshness. The early writers described the new sounds, sights, and tastes they experienced, and they passionately debated the issues raised by the presence of the autochthonous peoples of "the Indies," or *las Indias occidentales*, as they called them. Over the centuries, writers simultaneously reveled in, and muted, the apparent newness of their "new world." "Novus," or new, implied novelty as well as that which was newly found, and by the eighteenth century its connotations came to include "uncultivated," "not-quite-formed," and even "degenerate." Having begun soon after Columbus, the great debates about the old New World and its inhabitants again haunted the Americas at the time of the Enlightenment.

In an odd reprise of the sixteenth-century question of whether the Indians were capable of effective self-governance, the Spanish national legislature (*Cortes*) convened in Cádiz, Spain, during the French occupation, debated, in 1811 and 1812, whether the American viceroyalties' creoles were prepared to govern themselves. In its earliest post-1492 days the term "creole" (*criollo*) had referred literally to the first generations of sons and daughters of Spaniards, other Europeans, and Africans born in America. As the distance from ancestral ethnic homes and traditions lengthened over time, there emerged new varieties of "creole consciousness": cultural and patriotic self-identifications that demanded social recognition and ultimately political independence.

Politically and culturally, the colonial writers of Spain's America were connected to the metropolis, that is, the kingdom of Castile. This is where they sent their reports and manuscripts and published most of their books. Two sets of terms—the local and the metropolitan—were at play; this bifocal dimension of literary expression is a hallmark of Spanish colonial-era writing. Working far from the metropolis, these writers' authority was always open to challenge from the Castilian court or council chamber or other elite readers. As a result, their common strategy was to ally themselves with literary authority, with Pliny, for example, if writing about the natural world, with the model of Rome, if writing about Spanish conquest history, with Tasso and Ariosto if writing epic poetry, with Góngora and Quevedo, if writing baroque lyric or satire. These literary relationships were neither literal nor subservient, and the freshness of New World circumstances and the creative genius of thoughtful minds make these colonial writings stand out. It has been suggested, for example, that the Baroque in Latin America emerged not from Europe's models but from America's marvelous natural landscapes, its flora and fauna. Throughout more than three centuries of Spanish colonization, the perpetual quest of generations of American writers and thinkers was to understand and give voice to what the so-called New World meant—to itself and to the wider world beyond. Here all assumptions were repeatedly challenged, all hypotheses continually questioned. In America, all bets were off.

Of special relevance in 1492 was the publication in Salamanca, Spain, of the grammar of the Castilian language, *Gramática de la lengua castellana*, by Antonio de Nebrija. It probably appeared subsequent to Columbus's August 1492 embarkation in search of a western route to Asia, and it is popularly, absurdly *mis*understood as presaging the discoveries and conquests in the Americas. (It would have meant that the Salamanca Latinist was much more well-informed about uncharted waters to the west than Columbus, who died thinking he had arrived at Asia's threshold.) In his *Gramática*, Nebrija remarked that language was always the companion of empire and that language followed empire so closely that they originated, grew, prospered, and fell together.

Although the origin of his biological model was Lorenzo Valla's conception of language as an organic being linked to the life and death of empires, Nebrija's point was that the persistence of empire would be assured and made eternal by the art of grammar, recording imperial deeds in the vernacular language and preserving them for posterity. In his utterances about the laws the victor imposed on the vanquished, commonly "barbarous peoples and nations of strange languages," Nebrija had in mind the human spoils of war taken in the triumphal histories of the ancient Hebrews, the Greeks, and the imperial Romans. Following the Roman model of language and empire and expressing himself in a tone more Roman and bellicose than Castilian and evangelical, Nebrija's remarks about imperial and linguistic prowess referred to the threatening south rather than the unknown west: his projected point of reference was Spanish military actions newly in course in Africa.

In the end Nebrija's words came to ring partly true for Spain's experience in America. Language did indeed "follow empire" to triumph over the newly encountered Aztecs and Incas, and the notion endured in Spain's understanding of its own experience through the art of grammar in the Castilian language, that is, in the role the vernacular played in writing Spain's early transatlantic history and therefore in founding the literatures of the Spanish-speaking Americas. Unlike Nebrija's model, however, the Spanish language transcended the fall of the first Western early modern empire, and it prevails today not only in Latin America, including the Caribbean, but also in its worldwide diaspora.

The Castilian language and native Amerindian tradition came together in early colonial times through the interaction of indigenous Americans with Spanish clergy. Alphabetic writing was the colonial institution that accounted for and managed native societies, evangelized them, and documented their traditional spiritual practices. In Mexico, the lifelong efforts of the Franciscan friar Bernardino de Sahagún produced by 1580 a monumental study of Aztec culture, originally written in Nahuatl, known as the *Florentine Codex*. In Peru, the compilation of native traditions, written down in Quechua for the purpose of eradicating them under the supervision of the creole priest Francisco de Ávila, resulted in 1608 in the illuminating account of Andean spiritual life known as the *Huarochirí Manuscript*.

For such Spanish missionary inquiries into native tradition, the collaboration of native informants was essential. In Mexico, ethnic lords and their heirs were trained by Franciscan friars at the Colegio de Santacruz de Santiago Tlaltelolco. In Peru, similar schools (*colegios*) for the sons of native lords were organized by the Jesuits. But such training was ultimately limited. Hoping to create a learned class of native intellectuals and even ordained Roman Catholic priests, these early missionary endeavors prepared instead native scribes and oral interpreters to work as adjuncts in colonial administration; a few eventually became writers.

The independent use of writing in Spanish by native Americans emerged and yielded two types of written expression that were sometimes mutually exclusive and occasionally overlapped. The efforts to communicate the interests of native society to its foreign overlords in reports and chronicles written in Spanish were complemented, or countered, by the recognition that alphabetic writing could be used to preserve the record of native spiritual life and ritual, keeping it safe from destruction by the colonizers. The Maya-language traditions set down in Roman alphabet in such sacred and ritual texts as the *Popol Vuh* and the *Books of Chilam Balam* of the Quiché and Yucatec Maya, respectively, exemplify this phenomenon. Paradoxically, the use of written culture to suppress the native heritage also served to preserve its noblest fruits.

The preservation of oral traditions and the presence of orality in these written-down texts are both profound and elusive. The notion of the "transition" from orality to writing falsely assumes a substitution of one by the other that did not occur; the persistence of oral performance right up to the present day is well documented. It is impossible to imagine a colonial Latin American literary tradition untouched by the tangible and intangible presence of native Amerindian traditions, all of whose manifestations—as we know them today—were assembled after Columbus.

Many Latin American colonial cultural legacies will be familiar to the reader. They range from Taíno words that linger in our lexicon (tobacco, hurricane, hammock, canoe, barbeque, cacique) to the internationally assimilated, infamous Black Legend of Spanish history, that is, the anti-Spanish sentiment of fourteenth- and fifteenth-century European origin that condemned Castilian militarism, Catalonian mercantilism, and the Spanish heritage of Semitic and Saracen blood. The Black Legend made the Spanish Inquisition and the Castilian conquests in America the "proof" that Spanish history was blacker and bloodier than any other in Europe.

Circulating now as then, these topics have often been reduced to oversimplification, such as the popular notions that the conquistadores imagined themselves to be real-life heroes of chivalric adventure, that all Amerindians took the Europeans to be gods, and that Spanish soldiers and scholars alike considered the natives of the New World to be less than fully human. These themes have persisted because they rationalized events and outcomes too troubling if not too complex to assimilate. The examination of colonial Latin American literature in Spanish sheds light on and corrects these regrettable commonplaces.

Why colonial Latin American literature? Its fascination is invoked by recalling the surprised observation in 1524 by the Salamanca humanist Hernán Pérez de Oliva, who wrote, "We used to occupy the ends of the earth, and now we find ourselves in the middle of it, thanks to a twist of fortune such as has never before been seen." The authors who occupy these pages are those who recorded what it meant to find themselves in the middle of the world, be they Castilian or creole, prose writers or poets, as well as those of autochthonous Amerindian background, who also struggled to occupy—but from a different starting point—a central place in it.

Chapter 1

First encounters, first doubts

The weight and heft of the writings of Christopher Columbus (1451–1506) on the Indies should never be underestimated. His "Letter of Discovery," as it has been called, describes a nearly prelapsarian paradise, and it set the agenda of themes that would be repeated, transformed, challenged, and inverted over the subsequent centuries. Returning from his first voyage to America in 1493, Columbus wrote his world-altering letter from the Canary Islands to Luis de Santángel, King Ferdinand's Keeper of the Privy Purse and Columbus's major advocate at court. In it he extols the beauty and fertility of the flora and fauna, praises the good will and gentleness of the island peoples, and promises rivers running with gold. He emphasizes the natives' intelligence, demonstrated to him by their skillful navigation in the waters of the Caribbean, and he postulates that they readily will convert to Christianity, inclining them-selves to the service of the Catholic kings, Ferdinand and Isabel, as well as to the entire Castilian nation.

Columbus's chief mode of description is comparison: he writes that the trees of Hispaniola in November are as lovely as those of Spain in May. His very first act, he reports, was to take possession of the land and name the islands he had discovered. Columbus saw what he saw through his own eyes but also through the lenses of his readings and common folklore: he points out that he has observed no "human monstrosities" but has heard of people with tails (an echo of the travel tales collected in the fourteenth century under the name "Sir John Mandeville"), those who eat human flesh, and women warriors who live without men. More than emphasizing his expedition's accomplishments, Columbus boasts about its extraordinary promise of spiritual and economic gain, not only for Spain but for all Christendom.

Thinking he had arrived at easternmost Asia (*las Indias orientales*), Columbus combined direct observation with his vaunted expectations that included the stuff of myth and legend. His brief letter, published in Barcelona in 1493 and in some sixteen editions in European languages by the year 1500, serves as introduction and epitome of his accounts of his four voyages and other writings; it anticipates all the issues that would be raised about the New World and its inhabitants, and Europe's relationship to them, over the coming centuries.

Fray Ramón Pané (ca. 1475–98?), a Hieronymite friar on Columbus's second voyage of 1493–96, took a much more sustained look at the natives of the Caribbean, as he lived for nearly two years among the Taínos of Hispaniola for the purpose of evangelizing them. He describes their beliefs and behaviors in his *Relación acerca de las antigüedades de los indios* (Account of the Ancient Beliefs of the Indians). Completed in 1498 and first published in 1571 in the biography of Columbus written by his son Fernando Colón, Pané recounts his contact with the native lords of Hispaniola and of how he learned about their religion and laws, which they preserved in song, just as the Moors did in writing. These songs, *areítos*, were known by heart by the lords, who learned them in their youth, and who sang them to the accompaniment of a special wooden drum.

Pané acknowledges that his information about Taíno beliefs and their gods, the *cemíes*, is fragmentary, imperfectly remembered, and the object of contradictory accounts. What was first should be last, he writes, adding that he has recorded everything just as it was told to him and as he, by the best of his lights, has understood it. Pané thus initiates a series of inquiries into Taíno culture "against the clock": his few notable successors include Gonzalo Fernández de Oviedo and Bartolomé de las Casas, whose researches were carried out as the Taínos' precipitous decline due to violence, hard labor, and disease led to their disappearance. Pané's modesty about his accomplishments and these modest beginnings nevertheless open a path of inquiry into indigenous American custom and belief that will span the entire period of Spain's colonization in the Americas. In addition to the precious information he provides about a disappearing people, Pané's earnest admission about the difficulty of understanding other cultures is one of his most worthy legacies.

Unlike the report Pané wrote about Taíno religion at the request of Columbus, the accounts of the Milanese Pietro Martire d'Anghiera (ca. 1458–1526) were read by Castilian noblemen and Roman churchmen, including three popes. His *De orbe novo decades* (Decades of the New World), written between 1493 and 1525, tells of unfolding events in the Indies from Columbus's voyages, including a summary of Pané's account, through the conquest of Mexico. He has rightly been called the "first chronicler of the Indies," offering his learned European readers first glimpses of America's wonders and, by fifteenth-century standards, nearly up-to-the-minute accounts of unprecedented events.

Martire was the most learned of the chroniclers, and his broad interests were those of the Renaissance humanist: the expansion of geographical knowledge, the advancement of maritime navigation, and the revelation of the natural world were of as great interest to him as human affairs. Martire tempered the premises of the classical learning that guided him with observations reported to him by eyewitnesses, and he had an uncanny gift for getting at the heart of others' reports. He would be followed by equally great minds, but few would be as expansive in their interests or as disinterested in tone and temperament.

Martire achieves grace and balance in his Latin prose, which he augments with Hispanicizing neologisms and a subtle gloss of classical myth and ancient history. His pace is swift, his descriptions vivid and brief. He avoids withering judgments and offers the reader the clear-eyed expression of an indefatigable curiosity.

Martire was the first thinker to attempt to deal with the conundrums presented by the European encounter with these "new" lands and peoples. "New" was his choice of term (*orbe novo*), just as it was, around the same time, for Amerigo Vespucci (*mundus novus*). In contrast to Vespucci's notion of variety contained in the idea of *mundus*, Martire's "orb," circle or sphere, implies the idea of unity, and it bespeaks the fundamental belief that the new lands are God's creation and therefore that nature in all the world is one. Martire resists Columbus's claims about having reached the archipelago adjacent to Asia, and his incidental statement, "Colonus ille novi orbis repertor" (Columbus, discoverer of the new orb), perfectly limits the event.

In its cosmological sense, "orb" refers to the hemisphere, and "mundo" in its moral sense, to the lands found within it. The terms "new orb" and even "new world" were sufficiently ambiguous to accommodate several possibilities as to the identification of the newfound lands. As time passed, however, Martire considered but ultimately rejected Columbus's Asian hypothesis; only then does the concept of "new world" become a proper name describing a heretofore unknown, unforeseen geographical entity that rejects the classical model of the world as consisting of three parts.

Appointed a royal chronicler of Castile in 1520, Martire remarks that no one returns from the Indies without seeking him out to offer reports, and he cites his personal friendship with Columbus; his sources comprise a veritable "who's who" of exploration and conquest figures. Highly conscious of criticisms that he has not seen America firsthand, he acquits himself by citing the examples of Aristotle and Pliny: Aristotle described the animals that Alexander the Great's commissioned reporters told him about, and Pliny relied, too, on the accounts of others. Martire is humorously skeptical of accounts that seemed to him exaggerated or fabulous; after recalling Hernán Cortés's claim that the towers of the Mexican temples are taller than the bell towers of Seville, Martire remarks that the reader might wonder if Cortés has ever seen anything outside Spain. Dutifully communicating what he has heard about legendary Amazon women inhabiting the island of Matinino, Martire declares that he considers such reports to be fabrications. Only on having an account from a credible witness does he reintroduce the subject, remarking nevertheless that his informant has not removed his doubt on the matter.

Martire was seduced by the reported glories of the tropical Antilles' flora and fauna as well as by its native inhabitants. His gloss of classical myth is everywhere apparent. He compares, for example, the ritual singing and dancing, or *areítos*, of young island women at the court of Jaragua in Hispaniola to the classical divinities of the natural world and to Dryads, the tree nymphs who emerged from fountains in ancient myths: "Our men say that their faces, breasts, torsos, hands and other parts are very beautiful and of a very white coloring, and that it seemed to them that they were watching those very beautiful Dryads or nymphs sprung from fountains, such as the ancient fables tell." All that was missing from this Golden Age paradise—marred nevertheless by man's ruthless ambition, as Martire points out—was the arrival of the true religion.

One of the early readers of Pietro Martire's work was Hernán Pérez de Oliva (1494?–1531), whose *Historia de la invención de las Indias* (Account of the Discovery of the Indies) of 1528 took its narrative plot from Martire's first Decade. Oliva narrates Columbus's first three voyages and the rebellion of one of his island governors, Francisco Roldán; he ends his account of Columbus's actions with the admiral's threat to the Taínos prior to his third voyage's humiliating conclusion in 1498, when he and his brother were returned to Cádiz in chains. Oliva concludes his work with an account of Taíno beliefs and customs, the source of which was Martire's summary of Fray Ramón Pané's original account. This is the first of many chains of braided readings that link Spanish colonial-era writers to one another and thereby to the creation of their own authoritative literary tradition.

Unlike Martire's writings, whose purpose was to convey the news of events in America as they occurred, or those of Oviedo and Las Casas, whose personal experience and ideological interests drove their narratives, Oliva took a step back. He stands out as one of the first to reflect, in Renaissance fashion, on the meaning of the Castilian arrival in the Indies. "Invención" here means "to discover, to find," not to create, yet to make sense of what was encountered required a kind of creative act. Oliva's purview was typical of an Aristotelian Christian ethics that subscribed to natural law and its principle of the universality of human values. As he declared in his essay on the dignity of humanity (*Diálogo de la dignidad del hombre*): "Man lives like a plant, feels like a brute animal, and understands like an angel.... He has in his nature all these things and thus the freedom to be what he wishes."

In his *Invención* Oliva's focus is neither the grandeur of transoceanic navigation nor the spiritual destiny of America nor the feats of the conquistadores, which he regards as unsavory at best. It is, instead, the dramatization of moral considerations in the encounters, "conversations," between Europeans and the island natives. After his years in Rome and Paris, Oliva had returned to Castile armed with a typical Renaissance interest in cultivating and promoting vernacular languages: "to use well the language into which one was born" was his motto, and his translations of classical drama into Castilian constituted his surest apprenticeship. Eloquence in speech is central to his ideals, and he extends it to the Taínos. Appreciating Columbus's description of the Taínos' speech as pleasant and agreeable, Oliva, without firsthand knowledge, remarks that it was clear and well articulated. His mastery of literary expression shines brightest in his dialogic representations of speech, and although *Invención* is not in dialogue form, the speeches of its protagonists reveal his gift. Referring to the Spanish invaders, the Taíno lord Guarionexio laments:

> I have dealt with them in war and peace, with sternness and gentleness, pleas and threats, acquiescence and resistance, and in nothing have I been able to prevail. You see my kingdom filled with groans and tears, the virtue of women defiled, and the blood of innocents spilled; you see the children perish from hunger and, although the Christians are the cause, they show neither repentance nor compassion.

Oliva sums up the result in a single sentence: "Spanish avarice for great quantities of gold became such a fury that it destroyed the simple peoples who revealed those riches to them." Without directly raising a clarion call to remedial moral action, Oliva nevertheless displays the Columbian panorama and anticipates the writers of indigenous American tradition who will raise their voices and reveal from their perspective the local consequences of the "invention" of the Indies.

Around the time Oliva was writing his *Invención*, twelve Franciscan friars arrived in New Spain in 1524 as its first missionaries. Forty years later, in 1564, another Franciscan, Fray Bernardino de Sahagún, who had arrived in New Spain in 1529, worked with four Nahua collaborators, Antonio Valeriano,

Antonio Vegerano, Martín Iacobita, and Andrés Leonardo, to
write a dialogue that they represented as having taken place in
1524 between the first friars and the Aztec elders and priests.
Sahagún and his colleagues, some of whom had become writers in
their own right, recalled the efforts of the learned men,
tlamatinime, of Nahua tradition: they "caused the book [the
pre-Columbian codex] to cackle; the black, the color is in the
paintings they continually carry." Now the friar and his Nahua
informants turn to remembering more recent history, and they
re-create a scene expressing the Aztec wise men's grave fears and
doubts about the friars' demands that they abandon their sacred
laws:

> But, we,
> what now, immediately, will we say?
> Supposing that we, we are those who shelter the people,
> we are mothers to the people, we are
> fathers to the people,
> perchance, then, are we, here before you,
> to destroy it, the ancient law?

The Aztec lords subsequently convene among themselves, and the
doubts they express in remembered ritual strains are brought to
life by Sahagún and his colleagues:

> For a very long time, the discourse itself was made with
> great care,
> two times, three times, the words were made to be heard
> by the ones who offer incense,
> just as the divine guardians [the Franciscans] say them.
> And those who heard this were
> greatly disturbed,
> greatly saddened,
> as if they had fallen and were scared,
> frightened.
> However, then when the word had been born,

and after the discourse was unified,
it was resolved that the next day
all the men would go together,
would go assembled before the face
of the twelve divine guardians.

The gripping interest here lies in the elders' anguished consideration "for a very long time" of the challenge they face and the tone of resignation, not joy, that seems to accompany their acceptance of the Christian gospel.

Throughout the subsequent centuries, the doubts and denials expressed by indigenous Americans and their successors, and the determination of all of them to squarely face reality, will reappear, transformed by experience over time. Although the reader will meet only a small number of them here, their doubting voices stand as a reminder that indigenous Americans and their heirs are ever present in colonial Latin American literature, even when not speaking in their own voices, even when not explicitly reflected in the voices of others.

Chapter 2
Oviedo and Las Casas

Always seen as the personal enemies they were, the differences between Gonzalo Fernández de Oviedo (1478–1557) and Bartolomé de las Casas (1484–1566) were matters of their personal experience and intellectual pursuits. Las Casas, the son of a Spanish settler and *encomendero*, or trustee, of Indians and their labor, went to the Indies in 1502, at the age of eighteen, to work in his father's provisions business; he was educated by the Dominicans on the island of Hispaniola and in canon law at Salamanca. Oviedo arrived in the Indies in 1514 at age thirty-six with the expedition of Pedrarias Dávila (Pedro Arias de Ávila) to work as a mining inspector at Castilla del Oro on the Isthmus of Panama; he had spent his formative years in the princely courts of Italy and Castile. Captivated by America's natural world and aspiring to write its history, Oviedo's international interlocutors were learned Renaissance men of Italy. Capturing Las Casas's attention in the very year that Oviedo arrived at Castilla del Oro was a massacre of Taínos that Las Casas witnessed during Pánfilo de Narváez's conquest of Cuba. This focused his efforts on policy issues—the Spanish treatment of the Indians, and the prerogatives and limits of governmental policy—and his principal audiences were the Castilian monarchs, from Ferdinand to Philip II, and the members of the Royal Councils of Castile and the Indies.

The histories Oviedo and Las Casas wrote varied accordingly. In his *Historia general y natural de las Indias* (General [Universal] and Natural History of the Indies), part 1 of which was published in 1535 and reprinted in 1547, Oviedo placed America on a broad canvas and Castile at the origins of ancient history. In his *Historia de las Indias* (History of the Indies), completed around 1561 but not published until the twentieth century, Las Casas concentrated on post-1492 events and colonial practices. Oviedo published a portion of his Indies history twice during his lifetime; Las Casas expressly requested that his own be suppressed for forty years after his death. With respect to natural history, Oviedo immediately studied its wonders and contemplated cultural variation in his *De la historia natural* (On Natural History), or *Sumario* (Compendium), as it has been called, published in 1526.

Las Casas came later to natural history and the study of Amerindian customs. After initially including these topics in his *Historia*, he removed them and took them up again after 1550 with a polemical, theoretical purpose in mind. The result was his *Apologética historia sumaria* (Summary Defense of the Indian Civilizations), completed around 1560 and first published (selections only) in the late nineteenth century. Despite their ideological differences, and because of their complementary perspectives, Oviedo's and Las Casas's works constitute the foundation on which colonial Latin American literature would rest.

Oviedo published his *Sumario* to immediate success in Spain and among the learned circles of Italy. Oviedo's enthusiastic readers and scientific collaborators included the scholar and poet Cardinal Pietro Bembo, and the geographer and cosmographer Giovanni Battista Ramusio. Ramusio translated and published Oviedo's *Sumario* in 1534, and Bembo summarized it in print in the following years; in 1546 Bembo expressed the hope that the new edition of Oviedo's *Historia general* would soon be available. The *Sumario* and the *Historia general* eclipsed Oviedo's first book,

Claribalte, a chivalric romance he published in 1519 and later found to be an embarrassment.

Pietro Martire was never far from Oviedo's mind. Oviedo faulted the Milanese's *De orbe novo decades* for relying on the "false testimony" of his conquistador informants, for lacking personal experience in the Indies, and for being written in Latin. Oviedo assured his readers that if "Latinist foreigners" whom he knew but would not name had produced their works in the language (Spanish) of those who had spent years in the Indies, such authors would be disgraced as liars and frauds. Oviedo himself was criticized for not having written in Latin, and he vigorously defended his use of the vernacular: he cited the precedent of Old Testament prophets and New Testament evangelists, the presumed superiority of Castilian over all other vernaculars, his desire to write for those who carried out the great deeds of the Indies as well as the general public, his admission that he did not write Latin with the skill of Pietro Bembo, and his insistence that his highest consideration was the language in which the laws of Castile were written—that is, in Spanish. Why, he asked rhetorically, should his chronicle not follow those worthy models?

The years of 1499 through 1503 that Oviedo spent abroad in the service of Italian princes gave him the tools for writing about the marvels of nature and the vicissitudes of human fortunes. In addition to personal exchanges with contemporary geographers, historians, and cosmographers, Oviedo read the poets of the Trecento, notably Dante, Petrarch, and Boccaccio; the historians and humanists of the Quattrocento; the classics such as Pliny; and church fathers such as Eusebius of Caesarea. Oviedo received from the crown his commission as royal chronicler on August 18, 1532, after initiating the campaign himself with the support of the city council of Santo Domingo. Oviedo's writing is vivid and engaging at every turn, and his prose is peppered with classical references and personal anecdotes. Aware of the limits of descriptive language, he made drawings; some of his sketches, reproduced in woodcuts, are among the earliest printed images of the flora, fauna, cultures, and customs of the Indies.

Oviedo endeavored to achieve a profound unity between the empirical Castilian experience of America and the biblical, classical, and historical authority of sacred and learned books. With his readings of *De rebus Hispaniae* by the archbishop Rodrigo Jiménez de Rada, El Toledano (ca. 1170–1247), whom he names, and the widely read Pseudo-Beroso by "Annius of Viterbo," Giovanni Nanni (ca. 1432–1502), whom he does not identify, Oviedo synchronized the history of the Castilian monarchy with the history of the world after the biblical Flood. His articulation of ancient myth and natural and human history earned him the right to call his work a general or universal history because he looked back to the Flood and the Christian revelation.

Oviedo placed Castile within a cosmography that was somewhat familiar to readers of his time, a geography that was altogether new, and a history that began with the universal Flood itself. Geographically, he maintained much the same attitude as Martire, considering but never affirming Columbus's hypothesis that he had arrived in Asia. Oviedo rejected Martire's naming the newly found lands a "new world," asserting that the Indies were neither younger nor older than Asia, Africa, and Europe. Attributing Martire's assignation to the fact that the ancients had not included the Indies in the three known parts of the world, he nevertheless found Martire's denomination, "New World," to be correct only if interpreted as referring to the lands of which the ancients were apparently ignorant and "which we now see before us."

Paradoxically, Oviedo argues that the ancients *did* know about America. He links geography to his notion of the historical destiny of Spain, stating that he does not doubt that in ancient times the kings of Spain had known about or possessed the lands of the Indies. He conceives the history of Spain as beginning with the mythical kings who arrived with Hercules, the first invader of Iberian territory, and

24

those who succeeded him; he explains the ancient expansion to the Antilles and narrates the tale of its divinely guided recovery for Spain, centuries later, by Christopher Columbus and his successors.

To achieve this convergence of ancient lore and modern fact, Oviedo argues that the islands the ancients called the Hesperides were in fact the Indies, having been ruled by Spain from the time of Hespero, the twelfth king of Spain, dating back 1,658 years before the birth of Christ. Given that the current date was 1,535 years *after* the birth of Christ, it follows, Oviedo concludes, that 3,193 years earlier Spain and its king Hespero had ruled these isles, the "Hesperides Indies." His triumphant conclusion is that after so many centuries God has now returned these territories to Spain and that Columbus had been given the divine charge to seek what, in fact, he found.

Oviedo rejects the conceptualization of the terrestrial globe as "parts of the world," insisting that the proper way to understand it is as two halves, with Europe, Asia, and Africa constituting one half, and the lands of the Indies the other. In this view, the newly found lands and peoples augment and complete the known world. Bembo and Ramusio defended Oviedo's geographical ideas, and on the basis of his geographical data, Ramusio published in 1534 one of the finest maps of the New World in the sixteenth century; it accompanied an edition of the histories of Martire and Oviedo, and incorporated Oviedo's novel division of the world into two hemispheres, a notion anticipated by Martín Fernández de Enciso's *Suma de geografía* (Geographical Summa), published in 1519.

In addition to laying ancient Castilian claim to the Indies, Oviedo favored wresting Castile from the grip of its expensive involvement in the Holy Roman Empire. The ancient Spanish heritage carried a far greater weight, he argued, than Charles V's imperial crown, going back a mere half millennium to Rome, in contrast to the three thousand years that Hispania and its kings had ruled the Antilles. Language and empire were one, yes, but this "empire" was Castilian, not Germanic. As for the present time, Oviedo insisted, it should be understood that the Indies belonged to the crown of Castile, not to the Holy Roman Empire. He emphasized that the Castilian monarchy's territorial expansion in the Indies was to be credited not to the foreign-born Holy Roman emperor but to the heroic efforts of ordinary Spaniards.

Oviedo accompanied his account of ancient myth and recent history with that of the immutable and present world of nature. If he cast Castilian history as biblical and providential, he saw the hand of God most directly at work in the natural world, and he considered that the oneness of the world was proven by the variety of its creatures. Oviedo is the greatest of all the natural history writers of the Americas, and his deep and joyous engagement with nature's wonders shines through his vivid descriptions of living beings, often further enlivened by his personal observations: the consumption of the prickly pear will make your urine run red as blood; the flesh of the terrestrial/aquatic iguana is delicious, but the church will have to decide whether it can be eaten on Friday. If he sought the authority of Pliny from first to last, it was not for the purpose of servitude to ancient writings but rather the desire to update and transcend them.

Oviedo's deep interest in the natural world is one with his interest in its usefulness to humanity. Two of his drawings illustrate basic principles of his work. The hammock makes his point about the happy convergence of the works of nature and those of man: Oviedo tells how the hammock is made and hung, describes the natural materials from which it is constructed, and recommends the hammock to his readers as an innovation in sleeping comfort. The other is the pineapple. Here appears another of Oviedo's principles in his treatment of the natural world: averse to ascribing monstrousness to nature, Oviedo thus tempers the pineapple's apparently off-putting or even repulsive aspect with the conviction à la Isidore of Seville, the early-seventh-century Christian thinker and encyclopedist, that monstrosities are part of the Creation and not contrary to nature's design.

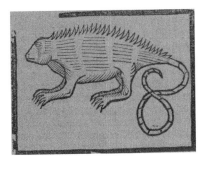

3. The hammock, the pineapple, and the iguana in woodcuts based on Gonzalo Fernández de Oviedo's original drawings, in his *Historia general y natural de las Indias* of 1535.

It is impossible to describe the pineapple without a picture, Oviedo writes, yet even this is inadequate for want of color. For those who have seen this magnificent fruit, he suggests, the image will be best augmented by that prior knowledge. For those who have not had that benefit, the picture cannot displease them if they supplement it with the written description in which he extols the marvels of the fruit as apprehended by the senses: its sight, its scent, its taste, and its touch. He advises that the pineapple's rough and prickly covering is best apprehended by being "picked up respectfully, with a towel or handkerchief." He assures the reader that, once in the hand, no other fruit offers such satisfaction. In like manner, the iguana may be scary to look at but is delicious to eat.

Las Casas sets a different tone. His concerns evolved from his initial attempts in 1516 to protect the Indians while ensuring the economic prosperity of the crown, to his ultimate recommendation, made forty-eight years later, that Spain abandon altogether its rule of the Indies. The object of his critique was the *encomienda* system whereby Spanish settlers were granted rights of trusteeship over Indians, obligating them to personal service and the payment of tribute goods. Under the private, domestic control of the *encomenderos*, or trustees, and without any recourse to higher authority, the Indians were effectively slaves. Three key moments define Las Casas's long reformist career. In 1516 he recommended alleviating the burden on the islander Indians by increasing the number of slaves imported from Africa and in 1518 he challenged the Indians' subjection to slavery and the *encomienda* system. In 1542 he proposed the abolition of Indian slavery and encomienda, which resulted in the passage of the New Laws that were ultimately rejected by governmental and private interests in America. Finally, in 1562 and 1564 he recommended that Castilian rule in the Americas cease and that sovereignty over all lands, possessions, and persons be returned to its native peoples.

The erroneous portrayal of Las Casas as the instigator of black African slavery in the Americas has colored the evaluation of his life and work since the eighteenth century. African slavery in the Indies had begun during the first decade of Spain's presence in America. By 1503 the newly appointed governor of Hispaniola, Nicolás de Ovando, whose 1502 expedition the eighteen-year-old Las Casas had accompanied to the Indies, requested that the flow of black African slaves to the Indies be stemmed because of their frequent, successful rebellions. Until reading Portuguese maritime histories in the 1550s, Las Casas labored under the common misunderstanding that the Africans the Portuguese imported as slaves had been captured in a just war, that is, in the defensive war against the Ottoman Empire waged by European Christendom. Upon learning that the Portuguese had hunted and captured peaceful Africans by plucking them from their homes, he acknowledged in his *Historia de las Indias* the regrettable role he unwittingly had played decades earlier: even though he had understood at the time that the Africans had been captured in the just war against Islam, he doubted now that his ignorance on the matter and his good intentions would spare him from divine judgment.

Las Casas's repentant recognition of the role he had played in 1516 in supporting African slavery reveals that, in his role as an historian of the Indies, his focus was always on history's actors, including himself. Las Casas's aim in the *Historia de las Indias* was to write the history of Spain's first six decades in America, through the 1550s. Although he started in 1527 and was still at work on it in 1561, his close scrutiny of Columbus's maritime and administrative career until the admiral's death in 1506 takes up approximately half the work. Equally detailed contemporaneous and subsequent events in the Antilles and on the mainland leave Hernán Cortés en route to, but not yet arrived at, the conquest of Mexico. Las Casas did not title his work a "general history" because, although exhaustive, it was sharply focused on a single question: How did things come to turn out as they did at the end of sixty years of Spain's rule in the Indies? He described the result as an "unprecedented casting off and diminution of the human race" for which Castilian governance of more than a half century's duration could not be held blameless before God.

Las Casas's final portrayal of Columbus reveals the issues he placed before the reader. For Las Casas, divine agency challenged humankind to exercise ethical conscience and to avoid succumbing to human frailty. From this perspective, there are no easy answers in his *Historia*. He narrates events but does not offer facile interpretations that the reader must accept or reject; he instead displays in sometimes excruciating detail the complexity of factors from which the reader must determine the causes and consequences of specific actions or larger patterns of behavior.

Las Casas's treatment of Columbus in the *Historia de las Indias* reveals that the Dominican examines history not with the certitude of his moral harangues but with perplexity at the great conundrums of Columbian history. Although Las Casas describes Columbus as a "good Christian," he shows him to have been caught in a web of conflicting goals and motivations. Columbus turns out to be neither the hero nor the villain of Las Casas's history, but rather a man who, like almost any other, failed to understand the gravity of the stakes of his actions or to anticipate the larger consequences and implications of his most mundane decisions. Columbus was an appropriate subject for reflection because his most casual dispositions contributed to chains of events that ultimately brought about, in Las Casas's view, the ruin of the Indies and its peoples, the never-before-heard-of diminution of the human race.

Las Casas's great proto-ethnographic treatise, the *Apologética historia sumaria*, shares a similar focus. The heart of Las Casas's analysis is natural history; he takes classical and medieval environmental theories and applies them to the Antilles, demonstrating that the archipelago was a most propitious place to favor humanity and foster the development of a benign human nature. Moving on to moral history, he uses the model of the city, derived from Aristotle and Saint Augustine, to define the civil order and ultimately to demonstrate that the diverse native societies of the New World had established bona fide civil societies. Las Casas follows Aristotle's *Politics* when characterizing the city as a self-sufficient social unit providing for the temporal, corporal, and moral needs of its inhabitants, including their protection from internal and external threats of harm. Las Casas combines this view with that of Saint Augustine, for whom the city embraced the life of a community, carried out in harmony and living in peace. Las Casas thus argues that the inhabitants of the New World satisfy the criteria by which social and civil orders are defined, even if their cities are constituted by districts and kinship groups and are made up of humble straw huts set together.

The most (in)famous book of the entire Spanish colonial period is Las Casas's *Brevísima relación de la destrucción de las Indias* (Brief Account of the Destruction of the Indies), printed by Las Casas in 1552 for a limited audience. Its origin was a report that Las Casas read before the Royal Council of the Indies in 1542 to persuade the councilors to abolish encomienda and Indian slavery. Based on testimonies about abuses committed against the Indians gathered from soldiers' and clerics' reports, personal interviews, and his own eyewitness accounts, this exposé and the attendant discussion resulted in the promulgation of the New Laws on November 20, 1542, which abolished Indian slavery and encomienda holdings. The provision ending encomienda was later revoked.

Pressing onward, Las Casas had his report privately printed ten years later for use by the Spanish missionary community and to spur Prince Philip, the future Philip II, to take remedial action. (Las Casas writes that the prince evidently ignored a manuscript copy received a decade earlier.) Although the *Brevísima relación* did not succeed in altering Spanish conquest policy or practice, it had a profound impact on the intellectual life of the times and afterward. It became then—and still is today—the most internationally known work in colonial Latin American literature and one of the most notorious pieces of writing in the Spanish language.

A dozen years after Las Casas's death, translations began to appear abroad. Ironically, the first two were concerned with Philip II's tyrannical policies and his minions' practices in the Low Countries: the Flemish and French translations of 1578 and 1579 were prefaced by the announcement that the conduct of Castile's soldiers in America should serve to warn the seventeen provinces of the Low Countries of their potential fate. This editorial event fueled the flames of anti-Spanish sentiment, the Black Legend, in Europe, and a staggering number of translations followed. By the end of the seventeenth century there were twenty-nine editions in Dutch, thirteen in French, six in English, six in German, three in Italian, and three in Latin. Their timing usually corresponded to the most critical periods in the wars fought between Habsburg Spain and its European enemies.

The *Brevísima relación* also became a bellwether of Spain's relationship with its American possessions. Its second florescence occurred in the late eighteenth and early nineteenth centuries, when the Dominican firebrand Fray Servando Teresa de Mier brought out editions of the work on three continents for the purpose of fomenting and seeking international support for the Latin American independence movement. After publishing seven hundred copies in London, Fray Servando followed it with editions in Philadelphia, Mexico City, Guadalajara, Bogotá, and possibly at the site of the Spanish legislature, *Cortes*, in Cádiz, Spain.

As an act of persuasion, Las Casas's language in the *Brevísima relación* is biblical, invoking Jesus's admonition to his disciples: "Remember I am sending you out like sheep among wolves; so be cunning as serpents and yet as harmless as doves" (Matt. 10:16, the Jerusalem Bible [1966]). When Las Casas thus compares the Indians to gentle sheep among the Spanish, whom he likens to cruel, long-famished wolves, tigers, and lions, he assigns the innocent good will attributed to Christ's apostles to the Indians. He compares the Indians' diet explicitly to that of "the holy fathers in the desert," implying as well the austerity of their dress and daily life. Whereas Oviedo had emphasized that the hammock was a felicitous innovation for the purpose of rest, Las Casas points out that pretentious conquistadores use them as litters in which to parade about like lords, held aloft by Indian carriers.

Las Casas's language in the *Brevísima relación* is also legal: he applies the principles of *jus gentium* (the law of nations, which natural reason establishes for all humankind) by which a government may not be imposed upon a people without its consent. He insists that the concept of conquest, that is, the legal repossession of lost lands and properties, is wrongly applied to violent acts of destruction in the Indies that he characterizes as acts of tyranny in violation of divine and all human laws. He refuses to acknowledge the resistance of the Indians as acts of rebellion, making the point repeatedly that since they have not submitted themselves willingly to new rulers, they cannot be considered rebels. If there is a just war in the Indies, he argues, it is that of the Indians against the Spanish.

Las Casas's language is also verbally—shockingly—visual. Proof is found in the copper engravings of Theodor de Bry's Latin translation of the *Brevísima relación*, published in Frankfurt in 1598, based on original watercolor drawings in the manuscript of an earlier French translation. The burning alive of native lords and the death by hanging of queen Anacaona capture the horrors of the conquest of Hispaniola. Terrified victims struggle to get free from this "mouth of hell" while a young Spanish page and an older peon bring wood and straw to stoke the conflagration. Natives in the countryside running away in terror are speared by armed horsemen, and a stationary figure in lordly pose, probably meant to depict the island's Spanish governor, Nicolás de Ovando, supervises the proceedings with satisfaction.

This image reveals the power of Las Casas's explicit and incandescent prose. The documentary source he followed in narrating his account was a letter of June 4, 1518, written by the Dominicans and Franciscans of Hispaniola to William II of Croÿ, Lord of Chièvres, one of the advisers whom the young king Charles had brought with him to Castile in 1517. The convergence in this image of art and event, deed and interpretation, characterizes the earliest colonial Latin American writing with its focus on the violence of war, the justice of which was the subject of long and keen debate.

4. The execution of Anacaona and the lords of Jaragua on Hispaniola in the Latin translation of Las Casas's *Brevísima relación de la destrucción de las Indias*, published in Frankfurt in 1598.

Chapter 3
The polemics of possession

Throughout the first century of Spanish colonial writing on the Americas, one fire would burn darkly and occasionally smolder, but would not be extinguished. This was the polemic concerning the right of Castile to rule the peoples of the Indies who had never invaded the lands of the conqueror, never attempted to supplant his religion with their own, and never wronged the Christian republic or refused to make restitution for goods taken. Because none of these time-honored, just-war conditions pertained, it became necessary to theorize, uniquely for the Indians of America, new protocols by which to wage "just war" against them. Positions on both sides of the long-lived controversy found their way into most literary and historical works of the early colonial period.

The issue of whether to govern and how to treat the Amerindians emerged during Columbus's second voyage, when in 1495 a shipment of Indians was sent from the island of Hispaniola to be sold as slaves in Spain. Ferdinand and Isabel convened a junta of theologians and other learned men to consider whether this was permissible according to the demands of Christian conscience. Reiterating a formal instruction of May 1493, the junta determined that only those Indians who ate human flesh, as reported by hearsay on Columbus's first voyage, could be justly captured as slaves. When the alleged cannibalism of the Caribbean

Indians was questioned by antislavery critics, an inquiry was authorized to call witnesses for the purpose of citing evidence about the practice. This hastily executed investigation broadened the range of legitimate offenses for which Indians could be enslaved to include "infidelity," "idolatry," and "the abominable sin against nature," that is, sodomy. The resultant "cannibal questionnaire," as I call it, of June 18, 1519, was used by Castilian ship captains and officers to justify the enslavement of Caribbean Indians on these more inclusive charges.

The specter of cannibalism helped turn attention away from the abstract consideration of the juridical right to invade the Indies and rule its peoples to focus on the capacity of the Amerindians for self-governance. The further twist was to assert the conditions by which to evangelize them: was it lawful for the Spanish king to wage war against the Indians before preaching the gospel to them? To resolve these conundrums, Charles V, following the model set by his grandparents Ferdinand and Isabel, convened a junta that has become the emblem of Spain's self-analysis on overseas conquest. In Valladolid in 1550 the emperor brought together the chief adversaries on the question: Fray Bartolomé de las Casas, who in 1542 had argued successfully before the Royal Council of the Indies for the need to reform colonial law, versus Juan Ginés de Sepúlveda (1490–1573), whose *Democrates Alter, sive de justis belli causis apud indos* (Second Democrates, or On the Just Causes of War against the Indians) of ca. 1545 advocating Indies conquests was prohibited from publication in Spain, thanks in part to Las Casas's intervention.

Essential to the Indies debates prior to 1550 was the theologian-professor of the University of Salamanca, the learned Dominican Fray Francisco de Vitoria (ca. 1492–1546). The Spanish university of those years was an influential institution, and the Castilian monarchs frequently called upon its most illustrious thinkers, Vitoria and his colleagues Domingo de Soto and Melchior Cano, among others, to offer counsel on such matters as the justice of the wars of conquest and the pastoral issue of the appropriateness of mass baptism of adults prior to their receipt of religious instruction.

More significant than his formal lectures were Vitoria's dissertations, or *relecciones*; this academic genre inquired into concrete points of a previously discussed topic and explored them in greater detail. In his *Relectio de Indis* (Dissertation on the Indies, or the Freedom of the Indians) of 1538, Vitoria focused on the issue of Castile's right to rule over the Indies. He did not accept the temporal authority of the pope to make donations of lands that were not under the power of Christian rulers because he understood the principles governing property rights in terms of lineage and succession, whose remote origin was the biblical tradition of Adam and Noah. He argued, however, that a secular prince could rule over foreign peoples because of their "natural need" to be governed by others. Although he acknowledged that before the arrival of the Spanish, the Indians had been legitimate lords of their domains and possessions, he cited Aristotle and asserted that there were those who were "slaves by nature," meaning that some were more equipped to follow than to lead, not possessing the qualities by which to govern themselves but only to follow the orders of their masters.

At the same time, again interpreting Aristotle, Vitoria took the position that limited intellect did not by itself deny the Indians the prerogatives of self-governance or ownership of their possessions. He invoked instead the right to evangelize them and the mandate to protect the innocent from such practices as cannibalism and human sacrifice. In Vitoria's view, the moral obligation of some was to exercise their God-given talent and rule over others, and for those others, moral responsibility consisted of accepting that imposition.

In his final dissertation on the subject of the Spanish right to make war against the Indians, titled *De indis, sive de iure belli hispanorum in barbaros, relectio posterior* (About the Indians, or the Spaniards' Right to Make War against Barbarians), Vitoria in 1539 drastically changed his view. He concluded that the sole just cause for making war against the Indians was to repel injuries received from them, and he cautioned that offenses suffered by the Spanish at Indian hands had to be very grave to justify such actions. At this point, Charles V brought to an end the role of these university theologians as advisers on royal policy, deeming that the complex, academic consideration of such issues presented more problems than it resolved.

Under increasing pressure from advocates of colonial reform to justify Spanish dominion in the Indies, Sepúlveda, humanist philosopher and Charles's imperial chronicler, wrote his *Democrates Alter* at the behest of the president of the Council of the Indies. He presented four causes by which to justify waging war against the Indians: (1) to impose guardianship, that is, the right and need to govern those who were incapable of governing themselves, the "natural slaves," or *siervos a natura*; (2) to abolish the crime of devouring human flesh; (3) to punish those who committed crimes against the innocent; and (4) to subdue peoples prior to preaching to them the Christian gospel.

The principles Sepúlveda elaborated bore strong resemblance to Vitoria's early thought. Their major difference was the degree of certainty each expressed: Vitoria equivocates, qualifies, and ultimately denies Castile's right to make war on the Indians; Sepúlveda categorically and consistently affirms it. Ignoring Vitoria's final retraction, Sepúlveda, in fact, asserted that Vitoria would approve his arguments while Las Casas declared that such an affinity could be explained only by certain erroneous conclusions drawn by the Salamanca theologian, conclusions occasioned by the "false information" Vitoria had received from others.

The stage was now set for the royally convened debate of Las Casas and Sepúlveda in Valladolid. The essentials of their thinking, inside and outside the formal occasion, concerned the temporal power of the pope and the Aristotelian principle of natural hierarchy. Sepúlveda followed the strict, traditional interpretation of the papal bulls of 1493 that granted Castile sovereignty over the lands discovered, in favor of temporal powers, interests, and duties. Las Casas rejected the principle of papal authority over temporal matters and interpreted the papal bulls of donation as solely granting to Castile the right to evangelize. On the question of natural hierarchies, Sepúlveda's position, like Vitoria's early arguments, adhered to the Aristotelian principle of the rule of the less perfect by the more perfect, such as the soul's rule over the body and reason over passion. He extended this hierarchical relationship, arguing that it should prevail "throughout the rest of humankind in its mutual relations."

Las Casas rejected Sepúlveda's philosophical arguments and appealed instead to the modern legal principles of *jus gentium*, by which the king's rule over his vassals rested on the voluntary consent of his subjects without carrying the force of natural law or absolute necessity. On this basis, the Dominican observed that while Sepúlveda alleged that the less perfect should, by its nature, always cede to the more perfect upon encountering it, this principle applied *only* when the two entities were found united in nature, "in actu primo," such as reason and passion, body and soul, matter and form existing in the same individual.

Las Casas rejected the extension of this principle to the relationship between different entities: "If the perfect thing and the imperfect thing are found to be separate and refer to different subjects, in this case the less perfect does not cede to the more perfect, for they are not united by nature, 'in actu primo.'" On this basis, Las Casas denied the possibility of a "natural" hierarchical ordering of the relationship between the Spanish and the Indians. Citing Augustine and Giles of Rome, he concluded that no free people could be obligated to submit to a more educated people, even if such submission would redound to great advantage for the former. In other words, he rejected the idea that the Aristotelian hierarchy could apply to "humankind in its mutual relations."

For Las Casas, the papal invitation to evangelize without force of arms followed strict protocols. He articulated his position, based on the Christian gospel, at the beginning of part 1 of his *De unico vocationis modo omnium gentium ad veram religionem* (The Only Way to Attract All Peoples to the True Religion) of ca. 1525. One might call it the doctrine of "shake the dust from your feet," and it appears in the synoptic gospels of Matthew, Mark, and Luke. Jesus gives instructions to his disciples as to the manner in which they are to go from town to town preaching:

> Whatever town or village you go into, ask for someone trustworthy and stay with him until you leave. As you enter his house, salute it, and if the house deserves it, let your peace descend upon it; if it does not, let your peace come back to you. And if anyone does not welcome you or listen to what you have to say, as you walk out of the house or town, shake the dust from your feet. (Matt. 10:11–13, the Jerusalem Bible [1966]).

In the foreign land the Christian is guest, not lord; abroad the Christian priest and the Christian prince are likewise outsiders.

Much like the civil law dictum of *jus gentium*, Las Casas also employed the basic canon law principle of *Quod omnes tangit debet ab omnibus approbari*, "what touches all must be approved by all." Developed to regulate the affairs of a bishopric, Las Casas applied it in the civil domain. As it would be dangerous to assign a prince or a bishop to a people unwilling to receive him, so, too, a foreign king should not be imposed on a free people. As a consequence, Las Casas concluded, the pope could not impose a foreign king on any people, Christian or non-Christian, against their will and without their consent.

Although Las Casas's authorities were scriptural and medieval, his vision with respect to temporal papal authority was unequivocally modern, combining traditional sources with current jurisprudence to render an up-to-the-minute view of Europe in its relation to the Atlantic world. Meanwhile, Sepúlveda had turned to ancient philosophy and medieval theology to support the characteristically medieval view that the pope possessed temporal powers over all peoples. In his Latin *Apologia* published in Rome in 1550, Sepúlveda accused Las Casas of provoking "a great scandal and infamy against our kings." Afterward, in his own, unpublished Latin *Apologia* of 1552–53, Las Casas accused Sepúlveda of "defaming these [Amerindian] peoples before the entire world." The official suspension of conquests was lifted and conquest activity was resumed—if, in fact, the moratorium had been observed.

In the wake of the Valladolid debate, the influential historian of the Indies Francisco López de Gómara declared in 1552 in his *Historia general de las Indias* (General History of the Indies) that any reader wishing to learn about the justice of the conquests could consult with confidence Sepúlveda's published works in Latin. In the same year, Las Casas published privately for the benefit of Prince Philip the work that would reverberate throughout the colonial centuries and beyond, the *Brevísima relación de la destrucción de las Indias*. The debate that in 1550 inaugurated the new decade was preceded by narrative accounts, such as those of Hernán Cortés, that took positions on its issues, and it would continue to reverberate, ever more pointedly, in the conquest histories that were to follow.

Chapter 4
The conquest of Mexico

Of all Spain's actions in the Indies, no event approximated the size or significance of the fall of Granada in 1492 until the conquest of Mexico of 1519–21. The application of the concept of conquest to America began with those events, when Hernán Cortés (1485–1547) exploited the reconquest heritage of Spain. Although "reconquista" was an eighteenth-century neologism, canonized in the nineteenth by the Spanish Royal Academy's dictionary, *conquista*, conquest, had much older roots; it referred to the legitimate seizure and occupation of lands, that is, the recovery of lost lands and properties from enemies of the Christian faith. The legitimate use of the term began to erode when carried from the Iberian peninsula to North Africa and especially to the Canaries, whose non-Muslim island inhabitants were innocent of such enmity.

For America the concept of conquest, inaugurated by Cortés, was canonized by Francisco López de Gómara. Bernal Díaz del Castillo also laid claim to it, and Fernando de Alva Ixtlilxochitl echoed it. Bartolomé de las Casas famously opposed the designation, pointing out its historical use and its only contemporary relevance: fighting the Moors of Africa, the Turks, and others who possessed Christian lands, persecuted Christians, or attempted to destroy the Christian faith.

Cortés's *Segunda carta de relación* (Second Letter of Relation), published in 1522, is the urtext on the conquest of Mexico. The most spectacular of the four extant of his five extensive letter-reports to the emperor, it describes the promise but not the completion of the conquest. Dispatched from Tepeaca, Puebla, in October 1520, after Cortés and his men were routed from Mexico Tenochtitlan on the fateful night of June 30, 1520 ("la Noche Triste"), the *Segunda carta* tells a suspenseful tale of co-options of enemies-turned-allies and military triumphs and reversals; it recalls the spectacular sights of the capital, and its chain of events has a human face: the capture, imprisonment, and death of Moctezuma, the head of the Triple Alliance of the city-states of Tacuba, Texcoco, and Tenochtitlan in the central valley of Mexico. A rhetorical tour de force, Cortés's *Segunda carta* had one goal in mind: to persuade the Castilian king, Charles I, newly installed as the Holy Roman Emperor Charles V, that despite Cortés's violation of the governor of Cuba's direct orders, his almost-conquest of this New World kingdom had been mandated by Christian providence and Aztec prophecy.

To this end, Cortés creates two speeches for Moctezuma. The first simulates the bogus Donation of Constantine, the forged decree by which the Roman emperor Constantine supposedly transferred his authority over Rome and the West to the pope. The Aztec ruler explains to Cortés that by virtue of ancient prophecy, "from the writings of our ancestors," Moctezuma and his people are foreigners in Mexico, that the authentic, native lord has departed, and that his descendents will return. Moctezuma gives the "keys to the kingdom" to Cortés, referring to him as the representative of those expected lords, and—this is Cortés's brilliant touch—applying to them the technical Castilian term *señores naturales* ("natural lords").

This concept had been used in Hispano-Christian states since medieval times to refer to those lords whose rule was based not on election or appointment by the community but on their status and authority as natives of the domains they inhabited; the people over whom they ruled were likewise native-born to the realm. Having Moctezuma call the Castilians the natural lords of Mexico, Cortés reiterates the principle in a second speech of literary ventriloquy. In it, Moctezuma explains to the native elites of the adjoining territories that the ancient prophecy of the return of their rulers has been fulfilled by the arrival of these strangers who are the representatives of the Aztecs' true and ancient "king and natural lord."

Enhancing this remarkable donation is Cortés's detailed, majestic account of the grandeur of the imperial city, the richness of Moctezuma's palaces, the variety of his amusements, and the hum and buzz of a busy, prosperous mercantile economy. This prose portrait models the splendor of ancient Mexico that López de Gómara and Bernal Díaz will seek to depict in their own works, and it will become one of the factors raising Castilian expectations about the promise of great wealth in the Americas. For Cortés the promise was realized. Although he did not receive the news in Mexico until May 1523, the emperor had issued on October 15, 1522, a royal decree recognizing Cortés's actions as a legitimate conquest and appointing him captain-general and governor of New Spain. (Cortés himself had suggested the name "New Spain" in his *Segunda carta*.) This was a novelty because at that time "Spain" as a legal or political entity did not exist, and—as Cortés well knew—the term "Spanish Empire" was a legal misnomer.

The consummate mastery of Cortés's narration is matched by the powerful graphic rendering of Mexico Tenochtitlan that appears in the Latin edition of his second and third letters published in Nuremberg in 1524. Like Cortés's letters, it combines empirical data with interpretive panache. The island city floats in its lagoon, and its neatly arranged buildings and towers likely evoked images of Venice in the European reader's eye. Yet the spectator's gaze is riveted to the center of the map, where a headless idol in human form is depicted with racks of skulls beneath its feet, suggesting the unspeakable horror of human sacrifice described in Cortés's account. Civilization confronts barbarity: Charles V's imperial banner flies on the mainland shore, poised to enter the central precinct of barbarity's realm to replace the headless, dismembered idol with Charles's imperial double-headed eagle. Although Cortés's victory in Mexico was far from assured when he wrote his *Segunda carta*, by the time of this 1524 publication the Triple Alliance had collapsed, having succumbed to Cortés, his men, and their multitudinous armies of native allies. The map, like Cortés's famous letter, celebrates the splendor and order of the conquered city as well as the most popular reasons, namely, cannibalism and human sacrifice, given as just causes for the war that defeated it.

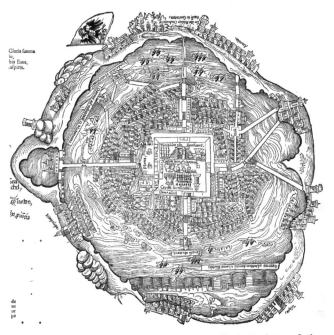

5. The map of Mexico Tenochtitlan that appeared in the Latin translation of Cortés's second and third letters published in Nuremberg in 1524.

Still, Cortés's victory was not without controversy. To the accusations and endless litigation produced by his enemies, Cortés would pose the learned, professional history, and thus Francisco López de Gómara (1511–59) undertook the task in his *Historia general de las Indias y la conquista de México* (General History of the Indies and Conquest of Mexico). Published in 1552, Gómara's magnum opus was quickly canonized; despite its ban in 1553 by the Royal Council of the Indies, it was successively, successfully reprinted. Supplementing the information provided by Cortés's letters, it offered the most sweeping general history of the Indies available at the time, and it was augmented by the first book devoted entirely to the conquest of Mexico. Like Oviedo, Gómara chose to write in Spanish for the benefit of the Castilian language, the glory of the kingdom, and the accessibility of his books to "all our Spaniards."

Gómara's style is among the most pristine of his peers. Eschewing long, Latinate utterances, his sentences are succinct, setting a laudable standard for clear and unaffected prose. Gómara sought to imitate the speech of the Castilian elite; he strove for "natural" rather than artificial expression, using the language with which one would "address one's neighbor," as the thirteenth-century Castilian poet-priest, Gonzalo de Berceo, had put it, and about which the Castilian Renaissance author Juan de Valdés announced, "I write as I speak." Gómara made use of proverbs and sayings for aphoristic effect and paired synonyms for emphasis. Like Valdés, he aimed to enrich the Spanish language by abandoning archaisms and employing neologisms borrowed from other languages. Anticipating the translation of his work (it would be published in Italian in 1556, English in 1578, and French in 1588), he lauded the Castilian language for its ability to accommodate profound and complex ideas in few words. The agility of Gómara's prose is one of his greatest achievements.

Gómara favored the theory of history in which the story of the lives, or the principal deeds, of great men predominated, and he viewed Cortés as one of the greatest men of modern times. Neither the generalized and impersonal ideology of conquest nor the royal prerogatives glossed in his account adequately took the measure of the feat; it was Cortés, the newly ennobled Marquis of the Valley of Oaxaca, whose intentions and actions exemplified the enterprise. Endowed by Gómara with peerless military judgment, strategic foresight, personal valor, and religious zeal, the figure of Cortés takes on epic dimensions and it would, in fact, inspire epic poems. Gómara and contemporary historians such as Francisco Cervantes de Salazar and Juan Ginés de Sepúlveda often compared Cortés to Alexander the Great, Julius Caesar, and Paul the apostle.

Gómara begins his general history with the announcement that the greatest event in human history after the Creation, excepting the incarnation and death of the One who created it, has been the discovery of the Indies. Expressing the conviction that history lasts longer than any individual's estate, Gómara adds the history of the conquest of Mexico to the great feats of human history and portrays the conquest of many and great kingdoms as a civilizing endeavor causing little harm and loss of blood to the natives: many millions have been baptized, he asserts, and now living as Christians, have abandoned human sacrifice and the consumption of human flesh. He lauds his fellow countrymen for willingly exposing themselves to hardship and danger and for being as committed to converting other peoples to Christianity as to conquering them. The acts of conquering and converting are all of a piece in Gómara's influential view, not only in the conquest of Mexico but in relation to the recovery of the lands of Spain as well: the conquest of the Indians takes up where that of the Moors left off, because, Gómara assures his readers, Spaniards are—and will—always be engaged in the struggle against religious infidels and pagans.

Gómara exercises independence of judgment about conquest events and expresses clear-eyed criticism of their protagonists' behavior. He condemns Pedro de Alvarado's massacre of the native elite at the *Templo Mayor* (Great Temple) in Mexico Tenochtitlan during the fiesta of Toxcatl in 1520, and he criticizes as cruel and tyrannical Cortés's treatment of Cuauhtemoc, the last Aztec lord to rule an independent Tenochtitlan. Perhaps against his own better judgment, Gómara thus reveals the profound human and moral cost of conquest. The publication in 2010, in English, of the Nahuatl translation of Gómara's *La conquista de México* by the seventeenth-century Nahua historian Domingo Francisco de San Antón Muñón Chimalpahin Cuauhtlehuanitzin shows that Gómara created an opening through which the Nahua historian could claim a stake in conquest history. The same may be said of Chimalpahin's near contemporary, Fernando de Alva Ixtlilxochitl.

Gómara's mono-focus on Cortés helped motivate Bernal Díaz del Castillo (ca. 1495–1584) to write his *Historia verdadera de la conquista de la Nueva España* (True History of the Conquest of New Spain) in the period from the 1550s to 1584; it was first published in 1632. As a foot soldier in the war of conquest, Bernal Díaz wrote from the position of being excluded from the written narratives of history in which he claimed a role, and he was eager to correct the view that the war had been won by Cortés's military brilliance alone. At mid-century, Bernal Díaz was also confronted by increasing criticism of the conquest wars that was being translated into legislation limiting the prerogatives of former conquistadors, now encomenderos who, as trustees of native peoples, depended for their livelihood on native labor and tribute goods. Because of the publication of Gómara's triumphalist Cortesian history, on one hand, and Las Casas's *Brevísima relación de la destrucción de las Indias*, on the other, Bernal Díaz saw his historical due as a conquistador being ignored and the integrity of the conquest, which he did not doubt, seriously eroded.

Bernal Díaz's relationship with Gómara was strictly literary; he criticized the professional historian for his lack of ability to appreciate the perspective of the ordinary soldier. Bernal Díaz's relationship with Las Casas was personal: they had met at a junta in Valladolid in 1550. This was not the famous Sepúlveda–Las Casas encounter that took place the same year to debate the rights of conquest. It was a separate meeting, called by the Royal Council of the Indies, to debate and set policy on the issue of perpetuity in encomienda grants, that is, the transferability of encomenderos' privileges to their heirs. Bernal Díaz's pro-perpetuity interests lost to Las Casas's anti-encomienda arguments.

Not surprisingly, in his *Historia verdadera* Bernal Díaz directly challenges and contradicts Las Casas's *Brevísima relación* accounts of key conquest episodes, which "the bishop of Chiapas Bartolomé de Las Casas writes about and never tires of telling." The old conquistador, in response, seasons his defense of the Spaniards' successful preemptive attack on Cholula by remarking that the Spanish soldiers discovered the Cholulans' plan "to eat our flesh: they had the cauldrons already prepared with salt, hot peppers, and tomatoes!" Such descriptive flourishes reveal Bernal Díaz's gift for animated storytelling.

Bernal Díaz's broader objective was to place New Spain squarely in the center of Spanish history and to insure that the importance of Mexico to Spanish interests was not eclipsed by the more recent conquest of Inca Peru and the discovery of its spectacular mineral wealth. His *Historia verdadera* is unique among histories of the conquest of Mexico because its narration spans events from 1514 through the early 1580s, when Bernal Díaz added the last emendations to his much-reworked manuscript. Notably, it includes accounts of events from 1517 on, when Bernal Díaz accompanied the reconnaissance expedition of Francisco Hernández de Córboba that reached the shores of Mexico at Yucatán for the first time.

Bernal Díaz's plain-talking prose is marked by the poignancy of recollection and loss and the vividness of dramatic personifications, such as those of Cortés's Mexican consort Doña Marina, better known as La Malinche, and the phantom shipwreck survivor Gonzalo Guerrero. Bernal Díaz's greatest achievement was his ability to create a literary voice to simulate his own flesh-and-blood personality. He portrays himself as the oldest surviving conquistador, aged and destitute, "with a daughter to marry and sons grown and with beards and others still to raise." (Some were no doubt mestizos, of mixed blood, offspring from his likely liaisons with Indian women.)

Seeking his place in history, Bernal Díaz lists all the battles in which he claims to have fought. After railing against Gómara and describing the coat of arms granted by the crown to Cortés and the images it bore of the heads of seven vanquished Mexica lords, he declares that like Cortés he, Bernal Díaz, is entitled to a share of the wealth represented by the seven kings' heads. He adds that the motto written on the culverin, 'I, second to none in serving you,' applies to him, too, for valiant conquest service. He gets his due indirectly and belatedly: Cortés's shield, with its encircling garland adorned by the severed heads of the seven Mexica captains, appears on the engraved title page of the *Historia verdadera*, published for the first time in 1632, a half century after Bernal Díaz's death.

Making an argument on behalf of himself and other "valorous captains and brave soldiers" for their inherited merits and performed services, Bernal Díaz asserts that the conquistadores of New Spain distinguished themselves much more than soldiers of earlier times. Having read the Castilian chronicles, he says, he has learned that many knights of old, beyond being salaried for their services, also received titles of nobility, towns, castles, estates, and lands in perpetuity. (To readers of *Don Quijote* it will be clear that Bernal Díaz was a real-life Sancho Panza, awaiting a prestigious governorship.) "Yet we," the old conquistador declares, "won New Spain without the king even knowing about it!" Here he follows Cortés's argument: Bernal Díaz and his peers boldly conquered

Bibliotheca Colbertina

HISTORIA VERDADERA
DE LA CONQVISTA DE LA
NVEVA ESPAÑA.
Escrita
Por el Capitan Bernal Diaz del
Castillo, Vno de sus Conquistadores.
Sacada a luz.
Por el P. M. Fr. Alonso Remon, Pre-
dicador y Coronista General del Orden de
N. S. de la Merced, Redencion de Cautiuos.
A la Catholica Magestad del
Mayor Monarca D. Filipe
IV. Rey de las Españas y
Nuevo Mundo N. S.

Con Priuilegio, En Madrid, en la Emprenta del Reyno.

D. Fernando Cortes.   P. F. Bartolome de Olmedo.

MEXICO.

6. Title page of Bernal Díaz del Castillo's *Historia verdadera de la
conquista de la Nueva España* featuring Hernán Cortés's coat of arms
(see lower left) with its garland adorned with seven severed heads of
Mexica lords.

Mexico, disobeying the orders of the governor of Cuba and complying with the higher, exalted mandate of gaining new territories for their king and converting new souls to Christianity.

Bernal Díaz makes strategic use of the books of chivalric romance. Recalling his first sight of Tenochtitlan some thirty to forty years earlier, he rhapsodizes:

> We were amazed and said that it was like the enchantments they tell of in the legend of Amadis,...And some of our soldiers even asked whether the things we saw were not a dream. It is not to be wondered at that I here write it down in this manner, for there is so much to think over that I do not know how to describe it, seeing things as we did that had never been heard of or seen before, not even dreamed about.

While this passage is often misread as meaning that Bernal Díaz and others imagined themselves to be living out tales of chivalric romance, this text instead provides author and readers with a common reference point, the books of chivalry. Comparing the wonders of the Aztec city with the marvels read about in fictional tales such as *Amadis of Gaul*, Bernal Díaz uses comparison—a common approach, starting with Columbus—to describe the extraordinary, nearly unbelievable but real panoramic vista displayed before him. At the same time, Bernal Díaz distances his chronicle from the books of chivalry. If he were to organize his history into one great conquest battle per chapter, it would seem, he writes, like a fictional tale and thus undermine his historical credibility. He further makes the point about historical fidelity by titling his work a "true history," precisely to highlight its difference from the "lying histories" of chivalric fiction. Bernal Díaz looked not to romance for exotic experiences but to the squarely historical medieval Castilian tradition for the hope of concrete reward.

Pursuing the twin goals of historical recognition and material reward from a different quarter is Fernando de Alva Ixtlilxochitl (ca. 1578–1650), whose Nahua forefathers had collaborated with Cortés in the conquest of Mexico. Alva Ixtlilxochitl was the great-grandson of the prince Ixtlilxochitl, the last sovereign lord of Texcoco. He served as a minor colonial functionary of Amerindian towns, and he wrote several historical accounts and the *Historia de los señores chichimecas* (History of the Chichimeca Lords) after 1615. Having read Gómara's *Historia general de las Indias y la conquista de México*, Alva Ixtlilxochitl created a Cortés of impressive evangelical accomplishments, employing the same glowing terms the Spanish historians had used in decades past.

However, Alva Ixtlilxochitl parted company with Gómara and the others by equally celebrating the great feats of his Texcocan forebears and by characterizing the war of Mexican conquest as "the most difficult conquest the world has ever seen." He may have been pleased with Gómara's accounts of mass Christianization and the Aztecs' postconquest abandonment of "cruel practices," but he did not accept Gómara's view of a swift and easy conquest. In his view, the Spanish historian had not understood the character of the war—which had been "so many against so many," rather than "so few against so many"—nor had he appreciated the praiseworthy qualities of the Mexican warriors.

Alva Ixtlilxochitl affirms that the member states of the Triple Alliance enjoyed an ancient, worthy civilization in their own right, then quickly accepted Christianity and assured the Spanish conquest of Mexico. Whereas most accounts of Spanish authorship, from Cortés onward, featured the figure of the incarcerated Moctezuma as proof of European cultural superiority and the site of Christian mercy, Alva Ixtlilxochitl casts a spotlight instead on the valor and virtue of native lords who made that incarceration possible. In his account of their origins, he emphasizes the institution of war as the traditional civilizing force of his own people: the great lord Tlotzin had taught his people to be cultivators of fertile lands, hunters of wild beasts, and husbands strictly monogamous, while at the same time creating and ruling over a sovereign realm that was "the most bellicose ever seen in this new world, for which reason they ruled over all others."

One point that Bernal Díaz and Alva Ixtlilxochitl had in common was to stress, from their distinct perspectives, the role of the collective as well as the individual effort in war; yet like Bernal Díaz, Alva Ixtlilxochitl's emphasis on the collective is realized through the construction of individual leadership and heroism. He tells how, even before Cortés and his company founded Vera Cruz on the eastern shore of Mexico, the prince Ixtlilxochitl had sent ambassadors to welcome Cortés, offering him an alliance with Texcoco in order to avenge the death of the prince's father, the lord Nezahualpilli, caused by Moctezuma's treachery. At another critical moment in Alva Ixtlilxochitl's conquest narrative, the prince Ixtlilxochitl captures the lord Cacama, and turns him over to Cortés, by which act "many great obstacles to the designs of Cortés and the entry of the Holy Faith were removed."

In Alva Ixtlilxochitl's historical account, the Texcocan prince always struggles to bring the subjects of his kingdom and those of more distant realms to the friendship of the Christians. In the final victory of the Spanish over Tenochtitlan, it is the Texcocans who supply food and necessary provisions to the conquerors, including twenty thousand carriers, a thousand canoes, and thirty-two thousand warriors, in short, "everything necessary to support so powerful an army, and all at his own cost and at that of his brothers, subjects, and other lords."

Like Bernal Díaz's *Historia verdadera*, Alva Ixtlilxochitl's chronicle has the effect of a *probanza de méritos y servicios*, that is, the certified testimony of witnesses to one's meritorious deeds and those of his ancestors, compiled on his behalf as a direct descendant of the indispensable princely ally of Cortés. At the same time, Alva Ixtlilxochitl's work speaks to the larger goal of asserting the historical and contemporary dignity of his people.

He passes over detailed accounts of the ritual aspects of Mexican warfare, acknowledging them only by noting that prisoners of war had been sacrificed to "false gods." His denial of the familiar stereotype of native treachery, cowardice, and inertia, plus his assertion of loyal service to the Spanish crown, give twofold significance to his claims.

To describe the difficulties of recovering pre-Columbian native history, the Texcocan chronicler tells how an old cacique, or ethnic lord, was asked to recount the story of the origin of the ancient prince Ixtlilxochitl.The old man replied, writes Alva Ixtlilxochtil, that a great eagle flew down from the sky and laid a large egg in a nest in a tree. After the proper period of time, the egg broke open, and the child who was to become the great Ixtlilxochitl appeared, literally "hatched from an egg." In response to the objection that this tale was nonsense, the old lord retorted that he would tell the same story again to anyone who asked, especially to Spaniards. Registering the old man's cynicism, Alva Ixtlilxochitl makes the point that native historical authorities often kept the truth of their history to themselves because they were never taken seriously, or were entirely misunderstood, by their colonial interlocutors.

Alva Ixtlilxochitl here gives voice to the themes of literal communication and broader understanding across linguistic and cultural barriers, as do his Peruvian contemporaries El Inca Garcilaso and Felipe Guaman Poma de Ayala. In defending their native heritage, each of the three performs delicate narrative balancing acts to resolve the tension between ancient American mythical beginnings and Christian providential endings. Doing so in the idiom of the conquerors, such native/mestizo writers embrace, with more fervor than most, the arguments about the unity of humanity espoused in earlier days by Pietro Martire, Pérez de Oliva, Oviedo, and especially Las Casas in his *Apologética historia sumaria*.

Chapter 5
A North American sojourn

Standing alone on the conquest horizon is Álvar Núñez Cabeza de Vaca (ca. 1485–92–ca. 1559). His *Naufragios* (literally, Shipwrecks, figuratively, Calamities; both meanings were common) is one of the most widely read and translated accounts of Spanish exploration and settlement in the Americas. This is due partly to its relevance on three continents: Cabeza de Vaca is commemorated as a conquistador-caballero in his native Jerez de la Frontera, Andalusia, Spain; his South American governorship is remembered at Iguazú Falls on the Argentine-Brazilian border; and his earlier North American experience is pertinent to Spanish borderland history in the U.S. Southwest and to all those who imagine or follow the romantic "Cabeza de Vaca slept here" trail across the continent. *Naufragios* tells the tale of the European and the African confronting for the first time the wilderness of North America and its native inhabitants.

Cabeza de Vaca was a *hidalgo*, a member of the social class that consisted typically of landed proprietors who, although without title of nobility, were entitled to bear coats of arms displaying their illustrious genealogies. Cabeza de Vaca's forebears came from such noble lines, and his historical roots have been traced to Christian caballeros who participated in the reconquest of Córdoba from the Moors in the thirteenth century. His particular distinction is to have been one of the few Spanish explorers and expeditionary officials whose Indies experiences—and reports of them—span both North and South America.

Cabeza de Vaca was appointed royal treasurer of the 1527 Pánfilo de Narváez expedition to conquer and settle *La Florida*, that is, the vast unexplored lands beyond the northern frontier of New Spain in North America. In 1520 Narváez had been sent by the

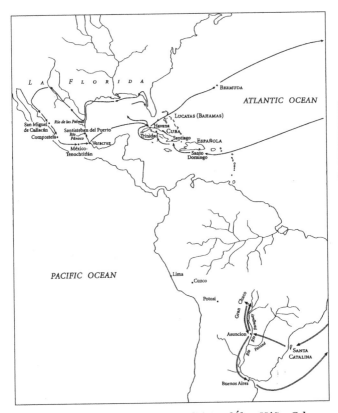

7. **The North and South American expeditions of Álvar Núñez Cabeza de Vaca, 1527–45.**

governor of Cuba to Mexico to thwart Cortés's illegal conquest
efforts. Defeated and imprisoned by Cortés and released five years
later, Narváez was determined to use his royal commission to
search for "another Mexico." This was a significant factor leading
to his expedition's colossal failure, because he led a force of some
five hundred men inland, into the area of present-day Florida, and
they were never reunited at the shore with the ships that were to
have waited for them.

After building and coasting in rafts across the Gulf of Mexico
from the Florida peninsula to the eastern shores of present-day
Texas, the five-hundred-man overland company was reduced to
four ultimate survivors: Álvar Núñez Cabeza de Vaca and fellow
hidalgos Andrés Dorantes and Alonso del Castillo Maldonado,
along with Dorantes's black slave from northwest coastal
Africa, Estevan ("Estevanico" in *Naufragios*). Of this major
settlement expedition, which began with nearly six hundred
persons, including ten Castilian women and an unknown
number of black African slaves, approximately ninety men and
the ten women survived by staying with the ships and sailing
back to Cuba.

For Cabeza de Vaca and his three companions it was a nine-year
sojourn, most of it spent stranded on the eastern shores of Texas.
The four men had endured slavery and hardship among the
Indians of the Texas coastal region for more than six and a half
years, and during four of those years Cabeza de Vaca was
separated from the others. After the four men's reunion and
escape in the summer of 1535, they journeyed overland on foot,
helped by native guides, emerging in 1536 at the Sinaloa River in
northwestern Mexico, where they encountered slave-hunting
Spanish soldiers. From the time of their departure from San Lúcar
de Barrameda in 1527 to their arrival in the capital of New Spain
in 1536, the world had changed. New Spain was no longer ruled
by the self-made conquistador Hernán Cortés but by an
aristocratic viceroy, Antonio de Mendoza, and controversy about

the justice and rights of the Spanish conquests was just heating up.

After he returned to Spain in 1537, Cabeza de Vaca sought another royal commission. As proof of prior service to the emperor he could offer only the account that has come down to us. It contains information about all he had observed and learned about the lands he lived in and traversed, their flora and fauna, and the "diverse customs of many and very barbarous peoples" with whom he had dealings and lived during the many years that he "walked lost and naked through many and very strange lands." Ironically, Hernando de Soto had just secured the coveted contract to conquer and settle *La Florida*, so Cabeza de Vaca had to make do with a commission for the less desirable governorship of Río de la Plata, headquartered at Asunción, in the heart of South America. His rule from 1541 through 1545 was a failure. Sent back to Spain in chains, he spent years fighting criminal charges that sprang from his conduct as governor. After his legal efforts exonerated his good name, he ended his career at the Castilian court, representing the interests of his natal Jerez de la Frontera. One of his last publicly documented deeds was to ransom a young relative held in North African captivity by the king of Algiers.

If Cabeza de Vaca's military career failed, his writing did not. The tale of his North American odyssey, published under the title *Relación* (Account) in Zamora, Spain, in 1542, was later re-edited and augmented by his secretary's account of his South American governorship. Published in Valladolid in 1555 under the title *Relación y comentarios* (Account and Commentaries), the work has been known popularly ever since as *Naufragios*. Read by information-seeking Spanish explorers and missionaries in the sixteenth through the eighteenth centuries, *Naufragios* has been studied by modern U.S. historians and exploration buffs from the middle of the nineteenth century onward.

In our own day Cabeza de Vaca's Pan-American experience has engaged the creative and critical energies of a range of Americanist interests—Anglo-, African-, Latin-, and Latino—as well as those of European scholars, translators, writers, and artists. They have set out and continue to explore the great themes suggested by the account: quest and adventure, freedom and bondage, empire and colonialism, miracles and shamanism. The healing episodes of the native infirm, described by Cabeza de Vaca in the fashion of Castilian *saludadores*, or healers, breathing on and blessing the sick or wounded, as well as his tales of the peaceful submission of native peoples to his party and his attempts to save the Indians from Spanish slave hunters, stand as narrative events that raise more questions than they answer.

Cabeza de Vaca is particularly good, however, at describing the mutual shock, surprise, attraction, and revulsion provoked by his own party, consisting of the white Castilians and the black African Estevan, in its encounters with the range of native groups from the Florida cape to northwestern Mexico. In this vast liminal zone Estevan is not a slave but the little band's chief communicator and negotiator, and Cabeza de Vaca the *hidalgo* becomes a merchant. Being alien to native society, the four men are often cast in the role of native women, that is, serving as messengers and traders of commodities, in negotiations between native communities. Crossing the continent in their final year in North America, he reports that they were considered as talismans, handed off from one group to the next as they traveled forward; most of all, they were perceived, he says, as beings of extraordinary shamanic powers.

The reader is propelled along by the tension of the narrative whose existence foretells its successful conclusion of homecoming after years of captivity. (This is captivity in its medieval and early modern meaning of being separated from homeland and everything one holds dear.) Still, it is a harrowing tale. The promise of, and threats to, their physical survival, reunion, and return to Spanish-held territory can drive the reader through the account in a single sitting. Haunting the narrative is Cabeza de Vaca's implicit suggestion that the four men's return fulfilled the pre-expedition prophecy of an old Moorish woman. More haunting still is Cabeza de Vaca's utter, predictable silence on what interests us today: the psychic dimension of his experience.

Cabeza de Vaca's prose does not sensationalize the very sensational events he narrates. His lexicon is straightforward, and his descriptions of recalled moments of high emotion are muted. Perhaps his greatest expressive verve comes in the tale of his seaborne homebound journey on a Spanish treasure fleet in 1537. French pirates pursue the Spanish flotilla, but it is saved by a Portuguese armada sailing home from India. In Portuguese, not Spanish, Cabeza de Vaca writes that the sea captain declares: "You certainly come with great riches, but you bring a very bad ship and very bad artillery! Son of a bitch, there's that renegade French ship. What a good mouthful she's lost!"

Despite this one ribald literary moment, *Naufragios* reads like an efficiently condensed and straightforward report, and it enjoyed great prestige for its authoritative account of northern lands, some of which would not be traversed again until a century and a half later. Early readers wove Cabeza de Vaca's observations into their own accounts, ratcheting up his modest and sober prose into episodes of heightened affect. Notable among them are Las Casas in his account of native religions in his *Apologética historia sumaria*, and El Inca Garcilaso de la Vega, describing the Floridian natives' predisposition to accept Christianity in his history of the De Soto expedition (*La Florida del Inca*).

The seeming simplicity of Cabeza de Vaca's 1542 and 1555 publications belies a narrative fully rounded but disconcertingly elliptical. The ever-unknowable quality of the experiences Cabeza de Vaca describes, as well as those upon which he does not comment, seem perpetually to stimulate readers' imaginations and make Cabeza de Vaca's saga relevant up to the present day. In his novel *El largo atardecer del caminante* (The Long Twilight of the Wanderer) published in 1992, the Argentine writer Abel Posse fictionalizes the experience of an aged Cabeza de Vaca. When the old explorer is asked if he does not have another version, perhaps a secret version, of his North American sojourn, he replies that he has "no patience for the prestigious lie of exactitude." In his 1969 short story "El etnógrafo" ("The Ethnographer"), Jorge Luis Borges creates a sojourner among native peoples who returns after two years in the wilderness, unwilling to turn his ineffable experience into the topic of a planned doctoral dissertation: "I possess the secret...the secret is not as important as the paths that led me to it. Each person has to walk those paths himself." As these works of fiction suggest, Cabeza de Vaca's unknowable experience and his account's mundane modesty keep *Naufragios* perpetually alive, continually read, and often reinterpreted, sparing it from the fate announced by its foreboding popular title.

Chapter 6
Epic accomplishments

As the sixteenth century gave way to the seventeenth, the crucial themes of the preceding decades were brought to a crescendo: a poet, Alonso de Ercilla y Zúñiga, celebrated in heroic verse the civic and moral virtues of an Amerindian people; a Jesuit priest, José de Acosta, did so in a treatise "in part historical, in part philosophical," as he called it; and the son of an Inca princess and a Spanish conquistador, El Inca Garcilaso de la Vega, who read and commented on the works of both authors, inaugurated the new century with a prose work that brought to its greatest heights the story of an extraordinary civilization and its demise against the backdrop of the ancient Andes. Ercilla, Acosta, and El Inca Garcilaso produced works that celebrated in their distinctive ways the achievements of the peoples of the ancient Americas and their descendents: one, an epic poem on war, another, an intellectual tour de force demonstrating the unity of the world and its inhabitants, and the third, a vast song of praise, in prose, to a thriving New World empire brought brusquely to its knees by Spanish conquest.

The epic poem flourished in the Hispanic world as nowhere else in the sixteenth and seventeenth centuries, due in no small measure to Spain's own "Americaniad," the epoch- and epic-making birth of the first Western empire in modern times. The epic poem still read today, perhaps the greatest of them all, is Alonso de Ercilla's

La Araucana (The Araucaniad). The son of a member of the Royal
Council of Castile, Ercilla (1533–94) became at age fifteen a page
to Prince Philip, the future Philip II, and spent several years in his
service. From Philip himself Ercilla obtained his license to serve in
the Spanish forces that attempted to conquer the indomitable
Araucanian nation that inhabited the area of present-day Chile.

8. Medallion portrait of Alonso de Ercilla y Zúñiga, author of *La
Araucana* and knight of the Order of Santiago.

La Araucana was published in three parts in 1569, 1578, and 1589, respectively. Some twenty-three editions of the work appeared by 1632, and it was heralded in the nineteenth century as one of the founding works of Chile's national literature. Its heroes and villains walked off the pages of Ercilla's poem and onto those of a bogus sequel, then onto the Spanish stage, and into ballads and opera librettos. Cervantes's *Don Quijote*'s village priest praised *La Araucana* as one of the three greatest works in heroic verse ever written in Castilian, capable of competing with the most famous epics of Italy. In his *Laurel de Apolo* (Apollo's Laurel Wreath) the Spanish playwright and poet Lope de Vega called Ercilla "the Columbus of the Parnassus of the Indies," that is, the discoverer, in America, of Apollo's sacred mountain devoted to the arts.

La Araucana is resonant with the legacies of Virgil for its martial dimension, Tasso for its religious content, Lucan for its historical interest, and Ariosto on love. Ercilla nevertheless considered the great Spanish Renaissance poet Garcilaso de la Vega his truest teacher. Garcilaso effectively launched modern Spanish poetry, consolidating the presence of Petrarchism in Spain that had been anticipated in fifteenth-century Castile by the Marquis of Santillana and that Garcilaso and Juan Boscán developed in the sixteenth century. Garcilaso perfected in Spanish the use of the flexible and elegant eleven-syllable line of Italianate verse form, thus augmenting the lively eight-syllable line and the ponderous twelve-syllable verse common to Galician-Castilian lyric. Garcilaso and Boscán cultivated the sonnet, the octave, and the tercet from the Italian terza rima tradition and supplemented the ballads and rhymed couplets of Castilian poetry with odes, elegies, and eclogues (Garcilaso earns sole credit here) of classical origin.

Romantic love in the tradition of Petrarch, unrequited and full of torment, or spiritualized and reflecting on inner sentiments, became a major theme; its literary expression relied on Greek and Roman myths and the wonders of nature itself. Against this background Ercilla selected as his poetic form the Italianate "royal octave" (*octava real*), a stanza of eight eleven-syllable verses that Garcilaso had utilized in his Virgilian eclogues. Ercilla made the royal octave his own, for *La Araucana* and the Castilian epic in general. Because of its rhyming pattern, *ababbcc*, with its first six verses alternating in rhyme and the last two verses paired, the octave was, in the hands of an expert lyricist like Ercilla, capable of economically producing aphoristic force, condensing the narrative or affective content of the stanza and making it satisfyingly memorable.

La Araucana was a literary triumph in the face of a historical failure: the Spanish did not succeed in conquering Chile. The work's historical content is minimal in comparison to its literary elaboration, and *La Araucana* offsets the account of the nonconquest of Chile with Spanish military triumphs abroad. Using classic epic motifs of the dream sequence, the descent to a pagan world, and prophecy, Ercilla narrates Philip II's victories over the French at Saint-Quentin in northern France in 1557 and the Ottoman Turks at the Battle of Lepanto in the Gulf of Patras in 1571. The poet's deepest reflections concern the triumphs and failures of the human spirit produced by war itself. Implicitly contrasting Philip's distant victories with the pathos of the local situation in Chile, Ercilla comments on the depopulation of Chile's vast domains and creates, for the purpose of expressing revulsion at them, gripping visions of the carnage of war.

Ercilla sought and achieved *admiratio*, that literary effect, so celebrated at the time, that was generated by the unexpected, the extreme, or by excellence. *Admiratio*'s essence was the exceptional: the production in the reader of reactions of surprise, shock, fear, wonder, or awe. "Admiration" in the English-language sense could as well be countenanced, but adulation alone misses the mark. The origins of *admiratio* are found in Cicero and include the appeal to the reader's emotions. *Admiratio* was often easily in conflict with the desire to create verisimilitude, the believable, which was required of the impulse to teach. Ercilla resolves this conundrum by placing his brave characters in the world of war, where the unbelievable is suddenly, inevitably real. He spells out this relationship: it is a matter of wonder ("cosa de admiración"), he writes, that the Araucanians, relying on nothing but their valor and determination, have redeemed from the Spanish and maintained their long-embattled liberty.

Ercilla's triumph comes not in his discursive reflections on war per se but in his creation of literary characters who are its heroes and victims—its human consequences. Ercilla's most memorable male war heroes are Lautaro, who dreams the same nightmare as his beloved Guacolda before meeting his death; Galbarino, who with arms raised exposes the stumps where his hands have been cut off, proclaiming that although defeated, the Araucanians can never be vanquished; and Caupolicán, the Araucanian general who, after years of fearless leadership, is captured, converts to Christianity and dies martyred, impaled on a stake.

Ercilla's heroines are modeled after Ariosto's, and he celebrates the faithfulness of one of them, Lauca, which leads to the epic digression devoted to the story of Dido, the founder and queen of ancient Carthage. This Dido is not Virgil's incarnation of monstrousness but one defined by patriotic sentiment and loving self-sacrifice. In Ercilla's verses Dido's foundational act provides an alternate model to conquest by force, and her suicide signifies the grandeur of Carthage, not its ruin. Yet perhaps the memorable figure, for producing *admiratio* as astonishment and shock, is Fresia, the wife of Caupolicán. Captured with her fifteen-month-old son, seeing her husband sequestered and in submission, she renounces him and in an act of cosmic vengeance hurls their little boy, the pride of Caupolicán, at his feet. With this act, the transcendence of Araucanian leadership is poetically truncated, even as the historical wars continued unabated.

Diego Santisteban Osorio's opportunistic follow-up, *Cuarta y quinta parte de la Araucana* (parts 4 and 5 of *La Araucana*), published at Barcelona in 1598, underscores Ercilla's poem's power. Only in Santisteban's pseudo-sequel does the poet-protagonist Ercilla kill an Araucanian combatant, only here do the Araucanians surrender, and here alone Caupolicán refuses to submit to the Spanish and takes his own life. Santisteban inadvertently reveals that part of the genius of Ercilla's work lies in the absence of facile solutions and expected endings. Ercilla's poem sublimely captures in heroic verse the trials and devastations of an unheroic era. *La Araucana* makes clear that the days of Spanish conquest glory like those enjoyed by Hernán Cortés in Mexico have ended.

While Ercilla seeks to locate the war in Chile on a plane with Philip II's wars in Europe, the Jesuit José de Acosta (1540–1600) contemplates the place of the Indies in natural and human history. He completes the cycle of inquiry regarding this "fourth part of the world" that began in 1493 with Pietro Martire d'Anghiera's *De orbe novo decades* and includes, among others, the works of Gonzalo Fernández de Oviedo and Francisco López de Gómara. Martire had simply assumed the basic unity of the Creation, with the new lands and its peoples being part of universal reality; a century later Acosta carefully maps out the theoretical and practical arguments to support it. The unity of America matters, in Acosta's view, precisely to understand its order, its rejection of chaos, and its purpose: the spiritual salvation of humanity.

Acosta performs an act of much needed synthesis. His *Historia natural y moral de las Indias* (Natural and Moral History of the Indies), published in 1590, examines the works of nature and, in the moral order, those of free will, that is, the works of man and, because it is "in part historical and in part philosophical," he advises his readers that his history can in some fashion be taken as new. It was immensely successful; two more editions appeared in Spanish in rapid succession and multiple printings of translations in Italian, French, German, English, Dutch, and Latin quickly followed. The clarity of Acosta's prose and the elegance of his exposition have been compared favorably to those of the great sixteenth-century Dominican devotional writer Fray Luis de Granada.

Acosta's *Historia* fulfilled a crucial need at the time. Once the surprise and shock of the existence of America as the fourth part of the world had been accepted, it was essential to systematically make explicit the implications of these unknown lands and their inhabitants. Acosta sought to demonstrate that America was not set apart from the rest of the world but rather that America, in all orders of its existence, was an integral part of the Creation. Thus he elected to substitute the concept of "continent" for the archaic "parts of the world" and made Europe, Asia, Africa, and America entities of a single type, with its beings—animal, vegetable, mineral, and human—likewise belonging to the same universal nature. Only from a moral point of view did America provide a difference. If, in the physical-corporal order, America was one among several continents, in the spiritual-historical order it was a "new world": a piece of inhabited universal reality hitherto unknown to Europe, an unforeseen possibility for its peoples' conversion to Christianity, and the prospect of their spiritual salvation as the providential fulfillment of human history.

The structure of Acosta's *Historia* reflects his ideas and beliefs, and constitutes the work's conceptual foundation, corresponding not to a mere inventory of themes but to an unfolding sequence of concepts. Acosta devotes books 1 through 3 to cosmology, geography, climate, and the four elements; book 4 to the animal, vegetable, and mineral world of the Indies; book 5 to Aztec and Inca native religions; book 6 to the proof of the Indians' exercise of reason via his discussion of Aztec and Inca calendars, writing systems, and governance; and book 7 to the laws, customs, and social order of ancient Mexico.

In these final books, Acosta's goal is to correct false popular opinions about natural limitations on the Indians' abilities and, in an effort to correct misguided colonial practice, he sets forth those native laws and customs that should be encouraged and retained. In this latter effort, Acosta relies on the offices of "most curious and learned men who have penetrated and understood their secrets," particularly his fellow Jesuit Juan de Tovar for Mexico and, for Peru, a colonial administrator, the *licenciado* (that is, university-trained) Polo de Ondegardo. He even cites Cabeza de Vaca's North American account as evidence of the natives' disposition to accept Christianity. Acosta thus simultaneously values empirical experience while engaging historical, philosophical, and theological authorities; his well-considered independence of judgment always shines through.

Among Acosta's notable readers, El Inca Garcilaso de la Vega (1539–1616) occasionally counters Acosta's views about Inca civilization on the basis of superior knowledge, sometimes identifying him and sometimes not. The *Historia*'s English translation of 1604 was excerpted by Samuel Purchas in his *Purchas His Pilgrimes*, published in London in 1625. Purchas does a comparative reading of Garcilaso and Acosta and cites their disagreements, often noting Garcilaso's corrections of Acosta with the marginal notation, "Acosta taxed." Purchas nevertheless considered the "learned Jesuite" one of his most admired sources, and this view was widely shared. He also cites the work of El Inca Garcilaso as one of the greatest "jewels" in his collection of Spanish New World writings.

El Inca Garcilaso de la Vega's *Comentarios reales de los Incas* (Royal Commentaries of the Incas), part 1 of which was published in 1609, part 2 in 1617, is the culmination of a body of work that spans Europe and America, postulating in narrative form the unity and integration of the author's bicultural world. (In this, he personalizes and historicizes the theoretical efforts of Acosta.) The complex irony with which Garcilaso refers to himself as an Indian belies his privileged childhood and youth spent in the bosom of his beleaguered but aristocratic Inca family while serving as secretary to his Spanish father, the royal administrator (*corregidor*) of colonial Cuzco, Captain Garcilaso de la Vega. El Inca Garcilaso spent his adult life, from the age of twenty, in Spain among his noble Castilian relatives, his learned Jesuit friends, and his books. In Córdoba and Montilla the ruins of ancient Rome and the Muslim caliphates surrounded him, and in his desire to prove his worthiness in the military tradition of the Christian caballero fighting against infidels, he took up arms in the war against the heirs of Islamic Spain, the moriscos of Alpujarras.

Distantly descended from the Castilian poet Garcilaso de la Vega, and taking his own father's name at the age of twenty-four, the former Gómez Suárez de Figueroa followed the poet Garcilaso's path by pursuing first arms and then letters, his life's vocation. The coat of arms he invented displays not only the symbols of his paternal Spanish and maternal Inca blood lines but also, using the poet Garcilaso's motto, his twin vocations of arms and letters. Here with less subtlety than in his prose we find a startling juxtaposition: the heraldic devices of Pérez de Vargas, Lasso de la Vega, Figueroa, Sotomayor and Mendoza de la Vega alongside sacred Inca symbols of sun, moon, rainbow, serpents, or *amaru*, here crowned, and the royal fringe, or *masca paycha*, worn by the reigning Inca.

El Inca Garcilaso produced three works that in hindsight served as preparation for his *Comentarios reales*: his translation from Italian to Spanish of León Hebreo's *Dialoghi d'amore* (Dialogues of Love), published in 1590, and a genealogical account of his paternal forebears, the "Relación de la descendencia de Garci Pérez de Vargas," completed in 1596 and intended to serve as a prologue to *La Florida del Inca* (The Florida of the Inca) but not ultimately included there. The latter work, published in 1605, was a history of Hernando de Soto's expedition to conquer and settle *La Florida*, the lands encircling the Gulf of Mexico and extending northward from New Spain. Although Francisco Vázquez de Coronado's expedition in the early 1540s resulted in today's

9. El Inca Garcilaso de la Vega's coat of arms, representing his Spanish and Inca lineages and his vocation of arms and letters.

southwestern United States being designated by the Spanish as "Cíbola," to El Inca Garcilaso, writing his *La Florida* in the 1580s, the extent of those lands remained a geographical mystery.

Seen from the perspective of *Comentarios reales*, this literary trajectory makes sense. Garcilaso's translation of Hebreo's synthetic, Neoplatonist treatise of 1502 helped him solve two theoretical problems: how to bring together elements of ancient pagan myth and the allegorical meanings attributed to literal accounts of historical events, and how to argue for the deeper meaning of myth without insisting on its historical credibility. Garcilaso studied how Hebreo's *Dialoghi* brought together ancient Greek learning and the biblical tradition and how they merged Plato's allegorical, mythical forms of understanding with Aristotle's systematic logic and encipherment of esoteric meanings. Hebreo's synthesizing conceptualization provided Garcilaso with a model for bringing together disparate Andean and Western ways of conceiving the world, human history, and time. That is, the Christian (Augustinian) march of lineal human history with its end in the salvation of humankind was at odds with the Andean model of cyclical time and human history's endless repetition of cosmic cataclysm and earthly renewal.

Garcilaso then complemented his theoretical apprenticeship with his historical interest in the comportment of the Christian cavalier from medieval to contemporary times. In his Garci Pérez de Vargas genealogy, Garcilaso celebrates the virtues of his paternal lineage reaching back to the thirteenth century; in his history of De Soto's failed conquest of *La Florida* he tells the story of one of his father's former comrades at arms whose meritorious military career, like that of Captain Garcilaso de la Vega, nevertheless ended not in glory but in obscurity.

La Florida del Inca spans the time period from De Soto's receipt of authorization from Charles V to undertake the expedition in 1538—the contract Cabeza de Vaca wanted—through the discovery in 1543 that De Soto and more than half of his expeditionary force had perished. De Soto had been one of El Inca Garcilaso's father's most illustrious companions in the campaigns of the early 1530s to settle Peru after its initial conquest by the Spanish. Ennobling De Soto's later efforts would surely enhance the historical reputation not only of De Soto but also of his compatriots and, albeit indirectly, El Inca Garcilaso's father as one of Peru's conquerors. Captain Garcilaso was in need of such rehabilitation, having been branded as a traitor in support of Gonzalo Pizarro's rebellion against the crown in the 1540s. In addition to Garcilaso's personal aims for recognition as a worthy cavalier's son, *La Florida del Inca* served the goals of celebrating the deeds of both Spaniards and Indians in the effort to conquer *La Florida*, giving the native Floridians their due as guides and interpreters loyal to the Spanish and portraying them as willing converts to Christianity—attributes he would later apply to native Andeans.

To dramatize his argument about the Floridian natives' peaceful submission to the Spanish, Garcilaso models episodes of Indian spiritual edification on accounts he found in Cabeza de Vaca's *Naufragios*. Because the De Soto expedition ended in disaster, as had the earlier Pánfilo de Narváez expedition on which Cabeza de Vaca served, the only possible triumph in both cases was spiritual. Announcing his Spanish/Inca background as pertinent to his stated effort to celebrate the deeds of both the Spanish soldiers and their Indian allies, Garcilaso's account allows him to defend the dignity of the native population and to echo the heroic sentiments of Spanish militarism in the service of the monarch.

His *Comentarios reales de los Incas* furthers these twin goals in the realm of the Inca. The panoramic canvas Garcilaso paints stands as the most complex and nuanced work—as well as the one written in the most polished, most expressive Spanish—of the entire Spanish colonial period. His hope would have been to create two ideal worlds: that of the just Inca and the evangelizing Christian caballero. In silent recognition of the impossibility of reality or history to measure up to such a perfect vision, Garcilaso imbues his meditation with extraordinary literary depth and pathos. He creates an atmosphere of emotionally charged recollection in episodes from his youth in which the poignancy of Inca loss predominates and in those of his adulthood, where frustration at his own circumstances appears, as in his encounter in Madrid with Fray Bartolomé de las Casas. (Las Casas had aided in the effort to successfully prevent Philip II from selling Peru to its encomendero conquerors, one of whose petitioner-promoters had been Garcilaso's father.)

El Inca Garcilaso's part 1 account of the Inca rulers' peaceful negotiations to bring other peoples into submission is countered by his part 2 narration of the chaotic, postconquest civil wars among the Spanish conquistadors and especially by his accounts of their failure to conquer Chile, for which he cites Ercilla's *La Araucana* as an authority. In a tour de force of accidental poetic justice, Garcilaso announces near the end of his work the death of the viceroy Francisco de Toledo, who had ordered the execution of the last Inca prince, the fifteen-year-old Tupac Amaru, known today as Tupac Amaru I, as well as the murder by Chilean Indians of Martín García de Loyola, grandnephew of the founder of the Jesuit Order and the Spanish governor of Chile, who had been Tupac Amaru's captor. Garcilaso's occasional turns to Chile reveal his quiet, ironic interest in the Spanish failure to conquer the Araucanians as just reward for having been responsible for the humiliating defeat of the Incas.

Garcilaso titled his work "Commentaries" because of its embrace of a long history beginning in Andean and Inca myth, ending in legally documented Spanish actions, and including an encyclopedic account of Andean institutions and customs. Like Martire, Oviedo, Las Casas, and Acosta, Garcilaso augments his account of human affairs (moral history) with that of natural history, describing in detail the flora and fauna native to Peru, as well as those species brought to the Andes by the Spanish. Still, his work is a commentary, not a history. With roots in antiquity and the Middle Ages, the commentary was recognized as an independent genre in the sixteenth century. Unlike a formal history, a commentary was free to add or omit the narration of pertinent events, and it was not bound by a single thesis or theme; ostensibly, its goal was to inform, not to explain or persuade. Its chronological limits were commonly the author's lifetime, and it served perfectly Garcilaso's highly personal essay on the topic of Inca civilization and the consequences of its fall, which he titled *Primera parte* and *Segunda parte*, respectively, to demonstrate the unity of the two parts of his work. He would have scoffed at the posthumously imposed, grandiose title of *Historia general del Perú* (General History of Peru) as betraying his more modest, though not immodest, intentions.

"Commentary" was appropriate to Garcilaso's method because much work in the genre was based on philological study (biblical and poetical exegesis), and Garcilaso claimed his knowledge of "the general language of Peru," that is, Quechua, and his explanations of its etymologies and usage, as the basis of his literary authority. Thus he described his book as a "commentary and gloss" on the histories of Peru written by Spanish authors whose ignorance of Quechua accounted, Garcilaso insists, for their many errors and misunderstandings of Inca religion, ritual, and history.

Translated into English, French, and German, *Comentarios reales* in the original Spanish was banned in Peru in 1782 as subversive, having been implicated as promoting the most serious native insurrection ever to threaten Spanish rule in the Andes, carried out under the leadership of José Gabriel Condorcanqui, known as Tupac Amaru II. El Inca Garcilaso's masterwork is taken today as the representation of an American consciousness, as a symbol of contested and conflicted concepts of cultural identity, and, more broadly, as an enduring, inaugural monument of the Latin American literary tradition. It would soon be followed by devastatingly critical accounts of colonial society that were often deeply satirical.

Chapter 7
Urban Baroque

The European literary and artistic phenomenon called the Baroque (etymologically, a misshapen pearl) has been defined variously as a historical movement, spanning the seventeenth through the mid-eighteenth centuries, or as an artistic sensibility and creative impulse that can occur in any period. As a style in the literary, plastic, and musical arts it is characterized by movement, contrast, exuberance, wit, and high drama. Its aesthetics consists of carrying to their ultimate consequences the artistic tendencies of the Renaissance that went before it. The representation of the world of nature is one of its most arresting topics. With the Baroque, for example, the sculpture of a tree does not take the geometric form of the column, as in Renaissance Doric style; instead, the column is transformed into a tree, as in the works of Bernini. In colonial Latin America the Baroque has been called *El barroco de Indias*, the Baroque of the Indies, and it has been characterized as the apogee of cultural originality in colonial Spanish America. Its distinctive feature is the convergence of three cultures—the immigrant European, the indigenous American, and the transplanted African—and it embraces the seventeenth and a portion of the eighteenth centuries.

In the plastic arts the Baroque's greatest visible legacy in Latin America is its great Baroque churches. These creations of

European and creole architects and indigenous American artists and artisans are, to the Western eye, at once familiar in architectural structure, yet new and strange in exterior and interior motifs and décor. The works of the eighteenth-century native Andean sculptor Kondori, who decorated the magnificent church of San Lorenzo in silver-rich Potosí, and the Brazilian mulatto architect and sculptor Antonio Francisco Lisboa, known as Aleijadinho and hailed as the master of the Minas Gerais Baroque, exemplify this achievement. This convergence of artistic styles and cultural traditions occurs in colonial literature, too, where popular and learned motifs, narrative, epic, and lyric impulses came together.

If sixteenth-century colonial Latin American literature is permeated by the polemics that accompanied Spain's taking political possession of the Indies, the colonial Baroque can be characterized as the endeavor to take possession of the Indies culturally, not only from without but, significantly, from within. The 1552–53 foundation of the universities of the viceroyalties of New Spain and Peru was complemented in the seventeenth century by the creation of literary academies and salons, or *tertulias*, and the ongoing study of America's natural world and native peoples. Spanish American creole and native writers began to take intellectual and literary possession of the domains they did not control politically, and Spanish immigrant authors, too, paid homage to their adopted land.

For all of them, "taking possession" included furthering geographical and historical knowledge of the lands into which they were born or to which they emigrated. The world of American nature was celebrated in poetry from the Spanish-born admirer of the city of Mexico Bernardo de Balbuena to the celebrated Mexican Hieronymite nun Sor Juana Inés de la Cruz. The creole polymath Carlos de Sigüenza y Góngora called startled attention to the glories of ancient Mexico when he boldly proposed that the newly appointed viceroy of New Spain should imitate the virtues of the ancient Aztec kings. Still, the culturally creole consciousness was a conflicted one. For those of European background, it meant celebrating the pre-Columbian past while holding themselves apart from its contemporary heirs; for those who identified with Amerindian civilizations and communicated with Western audiences, it meant either suppressing certain dimensions of their ancestral cultures or acknowledging and rejecting them.

If in the sixteenth century former conquistadores occasionally made the transatlantic crossing to petition the Royal Council of the Indies for reward, the seventeenth century was rich in transatlantic literary contacts. The book trade between Castilian printers and merchants and booksellers in the Indies was vigorous. It is still startling to realize that the bulk of the first printing in 1605 of Miguel de Cervantes's *El ingenioso hidalgo Don Quijote de la Mancha* arrived on America's shores within months of its publication. In turn, Cervantes's novel, and particularly his *La Galatea* (The Galatea) of 1583, registered Castilian familiarity with America's poets, revealing the connections that united the far-flung realms of the Spanish-language literary world.

In 1662 the Peruvian scholar and priest Juan de Espinosa Medrano passionately defended the poetics and poetry of the Spanish Baroque poet Luis de Góngora against a Portuguese detractor, and Sor Juana Inés de la Cruz corresponded with Pedro Calderón de la Barca and saw her poetry published in Madrid. The Spanish Renaissance and Baroque poets Garcilaso de la Vega, Fernando de Herrera, Góngora, and Calderón de la Barca were well known, admired, defended, and transformed in the poetry of their creole American peers and successors. In the best of cases, these ocean-spanning literary relationships produced results that were neither servile nor strictly imitative but rather were infused with the originality engendered by new circumstances, new insights, and new perspectives. If creole writers' literary attachments to Castile were significant, no less so were those established with the literary legacies of ancient Rome, whose achievements were also important touchstones.

One of the watchwords of the Baroque was the concept of *desengaño*. This is the phenomenon of the scales falling from the eyes, the coming to consciousness of the way things are, not as they are imagined or hoped to be; its strength lies in "knowing the score." Often misunderstood as disillusionment or disappointment—and it can lead to such affective responses—it is an intellectual, analytical phenomenon, resulting in the relief produced by certainty that, in affect and effect, can be either positive or negative. *Desengaño* can accompany or follow the experience of romantic infatuation and love, lust and adultery, or the revelation of tragic or tawdry travesties of justice.

Unveiling hypocrisy is an act of *desengaño*, and the laughter produced by satirical poets who gave the lie to social pretentiousness and puffed-up professional conduct—whether of prostitutes or physicians—can be heard from one end of the seventeenth century to the other, from Mateo Rosas de Oquendo to the great Juan del Valle y Caviedes. The laughter became deeply bitter with prose writers like Felipe Guaman Poma de Ayala and Juan Rodríguez Freile, who satirized and condemned the wayward ways of the colonial city. In a world ruled by those of noble Castilian pedigree, the concept of *desengaño* best captures the creole Baroque writers' certainties about their social and political limitations, and their sure knowledge that the exercise of sheer talent was the only way to proceed and, they hoped, prevail.

The Baroque frequently depicts urban life in the viceroyalties, and there *desengaño* rings truest. Writers portray the city as a site of political, social, and sexual corruption, and they make Lima and Santa Fe de Bogotá its most prominent exemplars. Both poets and prose authors display the city in the ribald language of its streets and the pidgin Quechua of its pulpits. Mateo Rosas de Oquendo's

Sátira hecha por Mateo Rosas de Oquendo a las cosas que pasan en el Pirú año de 1598 (A Satire Composed by Mateo Rosas de Oquendo about the Things that Happen in Peru, 1598) inaugurates the trend, revealing the seamy side of life in the colonial capital. Rosas de Oquendo (ca. 1559–1621) was a military man who received encomiendas in Tucumán and helped found the city of La Rioja; he also worked at the court of the eighth viceroy of Peru, García Hurtado de Mendoza.

Rosas de Oquendo's satirical poetry, like that of his successors, is topical and closely wedded to local circumstances. Expressed in local argot as well as in a learned, sometimes nearly esoteric literary idiom, his poetry employs the eight-syllable verse of the Castilian ballad as he takes the reader on an excursion through Lima's modest and mean streets. Anticipating Francisco de Quevedo's satirical, burlesque poetry by a few decades, Rosas de Oquendo's subject is mostly sexual, and his adulteresses, adulterers, prostitutes, pimps, and lowlifes are skewered for their vanity, deceitfulness, and roguery of all sorts. There is no respect for the aged; Rosas de Oquendo lampoons those libidinous oldsters who parade about like "mutton masquerading as lamb." He throws all castes into his melting pot: no pigment or skin tone is spared his wit.

The *limeño* satirist also takes aim at heroic epic poetry by mimicking and inverting the lengthy exordium and conclusion of Alonso de Ercilla's *La Araucana*. Ercilla's cavalier poet narrator concludes his epic poem alluding to the grandeur of his theme and lamenting his personal ill fortune; Rosas de Oquendo's pathetic picaresque narrator mocks that pose, decrying the world's vanity and his own, whining about his bad luck in life. Instead of Ercilla's poet's desire for arrival at a safe port, literally and symbolically, Rosas de Oquendo's *pícaro* declares that he is abandoning Peru and, in fact, condemns it to oblivion. His service to the viceroy Hurtado de Mendoza, who earlier had led the expedition to conquer Chile and become Ercilla's personal nemesis, may have piqued Rosas de Oquendo's interest in *La Araucana* and stimulated his exposés of the misadventures of soldier-conquerors, the emptiness of failed conquests, and the hollowness of their literary exaltation. Thus engaging the literary tradition of Castilian heroic poetry, Rosas de Oquendo suggests that its era is past.

Writing about Lima a decade or two after Rosas de Oquendo was the Andean chronicler Felipe Guaman Poma de Ayala (ca. 1535–ca. 1616), whose *Nueva corónica y buen gobierno* (New Chronicle and Good Government) was completed shortly after the end of 1615 and first published in the twentieth century. Although he was an exact contemporary of his compatriot El Inca Garcilaso de la Vega, his literary work does not share Garcilaso's Renaissance order and solemnity; he creates instead a baroque world of political chaos and social madness. Guaman Poma's multimedia, mixed-genre work may be considered baroque in the most raw and comprehensive sense of the term. His hellfire-and-brimstone rhetoric often leaves the reader staggering under the weight of the onslaught.

Guaman Poma was heir to a pre-Inca dynasty conquered by the Inca in the fifteenth century, and he also claimed maternal Inca lineage. He learned Spanish and became literate in Castilian, he says, through the good offices of his half-brother, a mestizo priest, and he was recruited in adolescence by Spanish clergy to assist in campaigns to identify and punish the practitioners of traditional Andean religion. This contact with missionary clergy probably provided the basis for his autodidactic book learning. He also worked as an interpreter in the colonial government's negotiations between European settlers and native communities, and his chronicle reveals that he knew the work of the Third Provincial Church Council. Convened in Lima in 1582–83 and presided over by the Jesuit José de Acosta, the Third Council produced a trilingual catechism and other devotional materials in Spanish, Quechua, and Aymara, and set policy to regulate the church's oversight of the native population.

Exiled in 1600 from the colonial city of Huamanga after losing a legal suit and being convicted of fraudulent self-representation, Guaman Poma went to live in a cluster of Andean settlements to the south that he had probably visited on ecclesiastical inspection tours. There, still in pursuit of justice, he appealed to a higher authority and by different means. He wrote his *Nueva corónica y buen gobierno*, addressing it to King Philip III, and traveled afterward to Lima to deliver the completed manuscript to the viceregal court for dispatch to Spain.

Guaman Poma's *Nueva corónica* is one of the most spectacular autograph manuscripts surviving from the Spanish colonial era, and its physical bulk announces the exuberant abundance of its contents, in prose and pictures, as well as its employment of elements from diverse literary genres. Pulling it all together formally are Guaman Poma's calligraphy and drawings. In eight hundred pages of prose he uses a Latinate form of cursive script derived from ecclesiastical models as well as roman-italic and gothic (black letter) lettering styles common to sixteenth-century type fonts and manuscript traditions.

His expressive but anomalous and sometimes opaque Spanish sentences are deeply inflected by his native Quechua and marred by errors in Spanish grammar and usage. Driven by his four hundred full-page drawings, his carefully planned and executed picture/prose ensembles variously convey similar information, explain one another, or stand in flat, mutual contradiction. Although it was registered in the Royal Library of Copenhagen catalog in the late eighteenth century, recent investigations by that institution have revealed that the autograph manuscript was deposited in the collections of the king of Denmark in the 1660s, a mere half century after its dispatch from Lima to Spain.

The formal perfection of the manuscript underscores its author's intended recipient: Guaman Poma envisions himself as the king's self-appointed advisor. For this purpose, the literary genres from which Guaman Poma drew inspiration are many: church inspectors' reports and how-to manuals, proto-ethnographic discussions of Andean rituals, customs, and institutions, exemplary Castilian biographies of fifteenth- and sixteenth-century vintage, Christian sermons designed to correct and condemn wayward conduct, the *santoral* or liturgical calendar, the lunar almanac or agricultural calendar, and colonial census reports.

The most significant literary models are Renaissance dialogues, the treatises proposing economic and social reform known as *arbitrios*, and the bodies of religious and moral reflections known as *Consideraciones* (Considerations). In the chapter he titles "Pregunta su Magestad" (His Majesty Inquires), Guaman Poma visualizes an audience with Philip and creates a dialogue between himself and the monarch in which the king asks probing questions about the welfare of colonial Peru's native inhabitants, and the self-identified "author and prince" lectures the king and provides the answers. His semi-prophetic "Considerations" are intended to complete the king's tutorial and save Peru's native peoples from destruction.

Guaman Poma calls his work a "chronicle or general history" because he conceived it as a universal history that followed the model of Augustine's ages of the world, beginning with Adam, and including a parallel sequence of Andean mythical history; Guaman Poma weaves together these strands so that they lead harmoniously to humanity's salvation. The Andean chronicler had read a sufficient number of Spanish conquest histories and works of Christian religious devotion and missionary instruction to transcribe or paraphrase them, most often without attribution. Most extraordinarily, he takes up the major principles of Fray Bartolomé de las Casas's *Tratado de las doce dudas* (Treatise of the Twelve Doubts) of 1564, then circulating in manuscript, and advocates, as Las Casas had done a half century earlier, the return of Andean sovereignty to Andeans. Closely following Las Casas's

10. In his *Nueva corónica y buen gobierno* Guaman Poma imagines, his book in hand, an interview with King Philip III and advises him on colonial matters.

model, he calls Philip III the "monarch of the world," defending the Christian faith and reigning symbolically over four sovereign and autonomous "kingdoms": the Indies, Christian Europe, Africa, and the world of Islam.

Guaman Poma's work is less a statement than a trajectory. What began as his hopeful, optimistic act of writing ends, with the final, autobiographical chapter, "Camina el autor" ("The Author Journeys"), as a record of despair, the ultimate *desengaño*: "There is no god and no king," he writes, "they are in Rome and Castile," meaning "there is no justice here in Peru." Satire is the channel through which Guaman Poma gives vent to and contains his rage. His satires are visual and allegorical, as when he employs the tradition of the medieval bestiary. Reiterating the Plautine topos, "man against man is a beast," an aphorism that became a common sentiment of the Baroque period, Guaman Poma's visual metaphors portray as monstrous animals the enemies of the native Andean: the encomendero is a lion, the parish priest, a fox, and so forth, recalling the language of Las Casas's *Brevísima relación de la destrucción de las Indias*. Most significant is Guaman Poma's parody of the sermon in Quechua.

Ironically, the sermon, the genre that provided his favored discursive mode, becomes, in his representation of local missionary parish practice, the target of his greatest scorn. When he simulates the preachers' voices, ridicules their stylistic mannerisms, and mimics their flawed Quechua, Guaman Poma brings to its darkest level his critique of the failure of evangelization because of missionary priests' ignorance of "the general language of Peru"—and their greed. Hopeful if not confident that he will have Quechua-speaking readers, Guaman Poma does not translate these satirical sermons into Spanish.

The degradation of Andeans by the colonizers nevertheless is bested by his account of rampant native corruption, like that of the co-opted local ethnic lord, the *cacique principal*, or the Andean woman who has abandoned her community to lead a wanton life in the capital. Guaman Poma reports that Lima is swarming with Andean village women, whom he describes as whoring and loaded down with mestizo and mulato offspring, all going about foppishly in fancy Spanish-style dress. The world, Guaman Poma repeatedly declares, is upside down when Andean women, who should be populating their villages at home, go about in Lima like poor parodies of Castilian ladies on the arms of Spanish or black African consorts. Satire is for Guaman Poma his last, desperate rhetorical resort, and nowhere is social chaos and moral ruin more on display than in the colonial city.

Also offering a broad overview of life in the city and its economic, social, and sexual corruption is Juan Rodríguez Freile (1566–ca. 1640), the chronicler-critic of the New Kingdom of Granada, located in the area of present-day Colombia and Venezuela. Rodríguez Freile was a creole native of Santa Fe de Bogotá who spent his life in the capital and its environs, managing his agricultural properties and researching the first century of New Granada's history. He was a voracious reader, and his personal library was filled with Roman classics and the works of medieval and Renaissance Spain. His reading took him to the municipal archives, and the single book he wrote combines tales based on mundane archival documents and edifying moral commentaries derived from his readings of Scripture and ancient and modern literature.

He titled his work *Conquista i descubrimiento del Nuevo Reino de Granada* (Conquest and Discovery of the New Kingdom of Granada). Completed in 1638 on the occasion of the centenary of the Spanish settlement of Santa Fe de Bogotá, it circulated in manuscript until the mid-nineteenth century. The title's reversal of the usual sequence, "discovery and conquest," suggests that Rodríguez Freile viewed the region's nearly bloodless conquest, which was based on the chimera produced by Spanish conquistadores' lust for gold and the myth of El Dorado, as a prelude to its still-awaited "discovery" of El Dorado's fabled riches. They were not found during the first century of the area's Spanish domination—and they have not been discovered to this day.

Rodríguez Freile catalogues the names and deeds of New Granada's conquistadores, settlers, and civil and ecclesiastical officials. He makes a point of identifying the descendants of those personages living in his own day, and he remarks with pride that his own parents arrived in New Granada in 1553, along with its first archbishop. Certain owners of copies of his manuscript book, whose ancestors were among the early notables, identified the work by a short title that has appeared in all editions of the work since the 1920s. This title, *El Carnero* (Dressed and Tanned Sheepskin), is found in only two nineteenth-century manuscript copies that coincide, significantly, with key events in the Latin American independence movement. One is dated 1812, the year that Simón Bolívar made the first major pronouncement of his revolutionary political agenda in the "Manifiesto de Cartagena" (Manifesto Pronounced at Cartagena de Indias), and the other carries the date of 1819, the very year Bolívar liberated New Granada from Spanish control.

As descendents of New Granada's earliest Spanish settlers and royal officials, the owners of these two manuscript copies possessed a genealogical treasure. Thus the enigmatic title *El Carnero* likely alludes to the genre of manuscript books, typically preserved in ecclesiastical or civil institutions of Castile, that listed properties and privileges of their jurisdiction's citizenry and were identified by their parchment (calfskin or sheepskin) covers: *carnero, becerro, libro becerro*. The privileged citizens of Santa Fe de Bogotá whose ancestors' names were recorded by Rodríguez Freile in his history of New Granada would have referred to their manuscript tomes as *el carnero*, taking pride in the old Castilian tradition even as they simultaneously heralded Latin American independence. (For prestige-seeking creoles, being able to prove Spanish lineage was always important, no matter what their political loyalties.)

Ironically, the content and thrust of *El Carnero* bespeak more shame than pride in New Granada's first century, which the author sums up in a lapidary sentence: "The fortified quarters of viceroys, governors, presidents, and judges cannot keep out amorous passions, because while those appointments are made by the king, these intruders come from nature itself, which has broader jurisdiction." In the archives Rodríguez Freile discovered that the public weal was compromised by peccadilloes of lust, jealousy, and deception, leading in some cases to exile, murder, or public execution and, in one instance, to a completely bogus, chimerical Indian uprising, thrown up as a smoke screen to cloak an illicit amorous adventure gone disastrously awry.

The tales, or *historielas*, of private, illicit sexual escapades are fundamental to the author's account of New Granada's public life. Lovers' deceits have brought the Kingdom of New Granada to its knees, Rodríguez Freile declares, as he surveys a Santa Fe de Bogotá riddled with holes in palace walls and other places, where broken marital beds and abandoned conjugal promises litter the streets. While these private peccadilloes have led critics to commonly read *El Carnero* as a "New World *Decameron*," Rodríguez Freile embeds these salacious episodes in intricate narrations in which the personal passions of lust or greed on the part of royal and ecclesiastical officials are shown to threaten the moral and economic ruin of the kingdom.

A case in point is the much-anthologized episode of Juana García, a mulatto sorceress who reveals to her mistress the adulterous life led by her husband in faraway Santo Domingo. But Juana had also divined the drowning at sea of the first two government officials whose civil misdeeds and punishment stemmed, not surprisingly, from sexual wrongdoing. When Juana is punished by the Inquisition for her witchery and exiled with her daughters from Santa Fe de Bogotá, she protests being scapegoated for the complicitous guilt of many fine ladies of Santa Fe. Juana García is not merely the protagonist of a tale about witchcraft and adultery; her figure is the narrative element that inextricably links the scandalous private lives and corrupt public dealings and disasters of the officials of church and state.

Although Rodríguez Freile never mentions the novel *Don Quijote* by name, as it would conform to the model of money-maker books, or *sacadineros*, that he dismisses as frivolous, Cervantes's novel provides Rodríguez Freile with a literary model for the expression of their shared sensibility: a criticism of human weakness that, if not pardonable, can be understood. He accomplishes this by using Cervantes's motif of the puppet show with its master and its stage director/announcer, or *declarador*. Rodríguez Freile remarks that "to understand this representation of the world, it is necessary that all the characters appear onstage."

With such expressions as "the conquistadores are shouting to me" and informing the reader that the generals "can wait no longer," he transforms the personages of the history of New Granada into puppets under his control. Like Cervantes's Maese Pedro, who distances himself from responsibility for his characters' actions by appointing a young lad to be the "interpreter and announcer of the mysteries" of his show, Rodríguez Freile, twice removed from the extravagances and abuses of his compatriots, can treat them with both humor and disdain.

The proof of Rodríguez Freile's reading of *Don Quijote* is revealed by his use of images and metaphors that have perplexed generations of the *santafereño's* readers. He describes his work as an "orphaned lass, virgin" (*doncella huérfana*), who, on the day of her betrothal and wedding (metaphorically, his book's public debut) must be adorned with borrowed clothes and jewels (his citations of canonical works and authors) and accompanied by flowers from the best gardens (popular accounts of local events, of which he chooses two: the Juana García story and that of the archbishop-Inquisitor who punished her). Should his readers be displeased, he continues, they can do as was done with the "bird of the fable," the Ethiopian phoenix of Herodotus. That is, although his book, like the phoenix, may "die" or at present be rejected, it will be reborn, or revived, by subsequent generations of readers.

The Cervantine link can be traced through the figure of the orphaned virgin. Cervantes so describes the genre of poetry in his novella "La gitanilla," and its fullest expression, as reworked by Rodríguez Freile, is first found in *Don Quijote*, where the figures of the orphaned virgin and the phoenix bird come together. Dorotea, as the Princess Micomicona, remarks to Don Quijote that being orphaned (*doncella huérfana*), her kingdom is being threatened by Pandafilando de la Fosca Vista. Don Quijote assures her that he would gladly save her from the fate of an invasion and unwanted marriage by marrying her himself, were it not for his devotion to Dulcinea: because of his lady he can marry no one, not even the "phoenix bird," that is, a creature so fine that it is unique to its species. From Cervantes's story of the Princess Micomicona emerge the images of the orphaned virgin and the revivable phoenix bird that Rodríguez Freile employs as a secret Cervantine signature to describe his own work.

El Carnero takes a definitive step out of the sixteenth-century exaltation of conquest that had been denied by Las Casas's *Brevísima relación* and eroded in Ercilla's *La Araucana*. Rodríguez Freile participates in the Baroque era's chiaroscuro shadings and its turn away from lofty promises to focus on trashy deeds and their long-lived, deleterious if not tragic consequences. From his perspective outside the circle of royal and ecclesiastical appointments and appointees, the creole Rodríguez Freile takes a distanced view of those who organize and control the kingdom. When he recalls from decades past standing on the docks at Cartagena and seeing great quantities of archival records and crates of gold prepared for dispatch to Spain, he remarks that the papers, representing New Granada's civic and moral losses, did greater harm to the kingdom than the draining of its gold: What is left in New Granada, he asks, that we may call it rich?

He sees only a ruinous society in which the lands of the great native lord Guatavita have been reduced to a single settlement and the forced personal service of the Muisca natives is a source of injustice and shame. The century that he describes as "golden" for the Spaniards has been, for the Muiscas and other native peoples, and perhaps for creoles, too, "a century of iron and steel." Among colonial prose narratives of the early seventeenth century, only Guaman Poma's *Nueva corónica y buen gobierno* delves so deeply into the failures of public life motivated by the greed for personal gain.

Like Guaman Poma and Rodríguez Freile, the poet Juan del Valle y Caviedes (1645–98) was a deeply critical observer of the colonial capital city. Born in Spain, he emigrated to Peru and devoted himself to commerce and mining; two relatives were judges in the viceroyalty's high court, and he married well, but like Rosas de Oquendo, his economic ambitions were unfulfilled. The ebullient life of the viceregal capital provided the canvas on which he painted his satirical portraits of prostitutes, false virgins, notaries, lawyers, physicians, and historical figures of his day, including doctors, royal officials, and even the viceroy himself.

Valle y Caviedes is the greatest of the colonial Baroque satirists, and his poetic language, like that of his *limeño* predecessor Rosas de Oquendo, consists of multilayered, nearly delirious wordplay and double entendres. Often faulted for failing to engage the Baroque luxuriance of the learned poetic language of his day, Valle y Caviedes, in fact, brings together two tropological systems, namely, those of poetic tradition and everyday life, with results that are both hilarious and cruel. Unlike Rosas de Oquendo, the breadth of Valle y Caviedes's poetic output includes religious, amorous, and moral poetry as well as poetic set pieces, or *bayles*, and brief entertainments.

Valle y Caviedes's major work is known today as *Diente del Parnaso* (The Tooth, or "Bite," of Parnassus), completed ca. 1689 but not published until the twentieth century. As with El Inca Garcilaso and Rodríguez Freile, the current title is a late imposition: Valle y Caviedes called his collection, "Guerra Física, Asañas [*sic*] de la Ygnorancia y Proesas Medicales" ("Physicians' War, Great Acts of Ignorance and [Other] Medical Feats"). He subverts the common formula of celebrating military triumphs (*hazañas*), metaphorically making the "feats" of physicians and healers, as peacetime destroyers, take the place of wartime conquerors. Valle y Caviedes's poetic proposal to send a fleet of physicians to defend Lima from the endless attacks of English pirates, his personalized invective against named officials of the viceregal court, and his attack on physicians' responsibility for the daily loss of human life encode a larger critique: the ignorance shared not only by Spanish physicians but by all immigrant Castilians to the viceroyalty regarding the climate, flora and fauna, minerals, and peoples of America.

Moreover, Valle y Caviedes's scorn is lavished not only on the deeds of deadly healers and quacks but more broadly on Scholasticism itself, the method of learning that relied on dialectical reasoning and formal disputation, and extended knowledge mainly by inference. Parodying its authority as outdated, Valle y Caviedes portrays physicians as relying uncritically and opportunistically on the authority of received, mechanical formulas while rejecting the modern approach to medical analysis based on the direct apprehension of observable reality.

"The Tooth or 'Bite' of Parnassus" alludes to Francisco de Quevedo's *El parnaso español* (The Spanish Parnassus) of 1652, and Valle y Caviedes's citation of Quevedo's poetry, as well as his own poetic range of topic and style, echo those of Quevedo's *Parnaso*. While Rosas de Oquendo depicts society's failings in a jocose, carnivalesque manner that softens the hard blows of the satirist's criticism via the self-parody of the narrative voice, Valle y Caviedes takes a more sober, moralistic approach that allows for no such mitigating reprieve—hence the appropriateness of the sobriquet, "Tooth or 'Bite' of Parnassus." Valle y Caviedes also participates in the misogynist tradition of the poetry of his era but takes it much farther, lampooning the myth of sexual excess and ridiculing the attribution of syphilis's origin to America.

No literary tradition or field of letters is spared Valle y Caviedes's wit. Its broad range and high moralistic content suggest that he strolled the streets, decades later, of Rosas de Oquendo's and Guaman Poma's Lima and gave full expression to the hypocrisy and pretensions of his day. Guaman Poma's foppish Andean "ladies" are superseded by Valle y Caviedes's creole *femmes fatales*, a few of whom are given, parodically, the name of Lisi, the beloved in many of Quevedo's love poems. The anatomy of one such deadly Lisi is metaphorically identified with the names of Lima's most infamous quack doctors, and her tale ends by taking a gruesome and deadly toll. In the depths of its satire and the heights of its moralizing, this dimension of the Baroque of the Indies, quintessentially represented by the poetry of Valle y Caviedes, is complemented by another of its faces: the focus not on colonial society but on poetic language itself as an object of contemplation.

Chapter 8
Baroque plenitude

The Spanish Baroque poet Luis de Góngora y Argote published his *Fábula de Polifemo y Galatea* (Fable of Polyphemus and Galatea) and *Soledades* (Solitudes) in 1612 and 1613, respectively, creating a poetic revolution that extended and transformed the Renaissance tendencies and traditions exemplified in the work of the Castilian poet Garcilaso de la Vega. With Góngora, the metaphor went wild, erudite words or expressions (*cultismos*)— often neologisms or uncommon, esoteric terms—bifurcated and multiplied, and mythical themes and motifs exploded. Góngora and followers of his style, called Gongorism, evoked Greco-Roman myth, history, and legend, commonplaces of philosophy and Ptolemaic cosmology, and rarities of natural history and other branches of learning, wrapping them all in dazzling images. These included rare fragrances, luxurious fabrics, precious stones and minerals, and flora and fauna, mythical, metamorphosed, or real.

This idiom, especially common in poetry, required ingenuity in its handling. Wit was expressed in conceits, and wordplay designed to startle and entertain has been cited as the Baroque's fundamental figure of thought. Writers associated terms typically unrelated or even pertaining to different orders of phenomena to render the familiar unfamiliar and to express in infinitely varied ways the finite world of objects and feelings. In his 1961 essay

"Homenaje a don Luis de Góngora" (Homage to Don Luis de Góngora), Jorge Luis Borges declared that Góngora inhabited the world of words more fully than any other poet, and he asserted that even Góngora's metaphors did not necessarily compare one thing to another but rather simply "moved one word near to another, which is different."

Nothing in Hispanic poetry would ever be the same again. Góngora's *Polifemo* and *Soledades* were his manifesto. From Ovid came the theme of the giant cyclops Polyphemus and his violent attack on the lover of Galatea, transforming him into a rivulet. The first *Soledad* starts with a shipwreck victim, washed up on a foreign strand, observing a rustic villagers' wedding. He stands back, as though all he sees is alien to him while still remembering, Petrarch-style, his own lost love. Góngora was attacked for his works' opaqueness and unintelligibility, and his works were the object of parodic imitations. Yet he was heartily embraced in colonial Latin America, where his books arrived with the semi-annual flotilla from Spain. The learned Peruvian creole priest Juan de Espinosa Medrano wrote a learned and passionate defense of his work; the renowned Mexican lyrical poet Sor Juana Inés de la Cruz glossed and rewrote his sonnets. The Mexican polymath Carlos de Sigüenza y Góngora, proud to share his surname, was also one of his admirers.

An exact contemporary of Luis de Góngora, Bernardo de Balbuena (ca. 1562–1627) may be said to initiate the Baroque of the Indies. He was not the most likely poet to celebrate the grandeur of the viceroyalty of New Spain's capital. Born in Valdepeñas, La Mancha, Balbuena emigrated to America and ended his career as the first bishop of Puerto Rico. He spent little time in Mexico, but his appreciation of its lush central valley and its bustling capital led to his most remembered composition, *Grandeza Mexicana* (Mexican Grandeur) of 1604. Balbuena paid homage to Mexico and to the pastoral literary tradition in his *Siglo de Oro de las selvas de Erífile* (The Golden Age of Heriphile's [the Sibyl Erythraea's] Forest Glens) of 1608. There the Mexican capital, like pastoral novels then in vogue, is wrapped in a magical dream world. He was equally fascinated by chivalric themes. His notable epic poem, *El Bernardo o Victoria de Roncesvalles* (The Bernardiad or Victory at Roncesvalles) of 1624 celebrates Iberia's resistance to the invasion of Charlemagne. Balbuena, in short, embraced with gusto and success the literary tendencies of his period.

He also presented its newest theme: a glittering, New World city, the heart of civilization, settled nearly a century earlier on the visible, still-present foundations of the pre-Columbian Aztec capital of Mexico Tenochtitlan. Seeing the variety and abundance of international goods flowing from coast to coast through New Spain and its capital, and also recalling Hernán Cortés's account of the Aztec city's great markets, Balbuena updates Hernán Pérez de Oliva's observation of 1524 about finding Spain at the center of the world. Balbuena presents a new image: Mexico as the world's center. At the halfway point between Europe and East Asia as well as being the hub of the outlying territories' regional markets from northern Mexico to Central America, Mexico City was literally the world's emporium. New Spain, Balbuena proclaims, divides the world into equal parts with the earth itself paying homage to Mexico, as though the city were a sun at the center of its own universe.

In moving from Bernardo de Balbuena's *Grandeza mexicana* to Góngora's first *Soledad*, the reader passes from a magnificent city to a bucolic meadow, from a peace whose troubles are no greater than those of love to a peace colored by the distant reminder of the ruins of war, from the exercise of healthy economic interest to that of ruinous individual greed, from the celebration of a glittering universal empire at its apogee to a sober reflection on the human cost of imperial ambition. While Góngora gives sublime expression to the *desengaño* of the Baroque, Balbuena pens a celebratory hymn of praise.

Dedicated to the archbishop of New Spain, *Grandeza mexicana* is presented as a "letter" to Isabel de Tovar y Guzmán, granddaughter of a lady-in-waiting to Queen Juana and a relative of Philip III's trusted courtier-confidante, the duke of Lerma. The poem opens with a hendecasyllabic *octava real*, that is, a stanza of eight eleven-syllable lines, the verses of which become the titles of eight of the work's nine chapters. The poet promises Doña Isabel that everything worth knowing about the viceregal city is therein summarized and encoded ("cifrado"). One of its most luminous chapters celebrates the world of nature. "Primavera inmortal y sus indicios" captivated a literary mind no less than that of Samuel Beckett, who rendered it in English as "Immortal Springtime and Its Tokens."

Tempe, a valley in Thessaly, "so celebrated in Greek eloquence, with more of wit and elegance than just cause," cannot compete with the magnificent central valley of Mexico; Tempe is but a "jot and tittle beside the flowering Mexican domain." The illustrious city, protected by heaven and its favors, lacks nothing "save Mars and his disturbances" and lives "in peace (if it be that love is not warfare)." Balbuena had commented on the poetry of Luis de Góngora in 1604, and Balbuena's analogy of love and war in *Grandeza mexicana* anticipates but does not match the brilliance of the final verse of Góngora's "Soledad primera" (First Solitude) of 1613: "A batallas de amor campos de pluma" ("for battles of love, a field of feathers"), in reference to the featherbed battleground of lovers.

A celebrated creole defender of the poetry of Góngora is Juan de Espinosa Medrano (1632–88), called "Lunarejo" because of a facial birthmark (*lunar* = mole) but also honored by his contemporaries with the flattering epithet "Sublime Doctor." A Peruvian creole priest whose sermons were published posthumously in Spain in 1699, Espinosa Medrano figures prominently in the literary Baroque of the Indies. Studying an attack on Góngora's poetry published decades earlier by a Portuguese defender of Camões,

Manuel de Faria, Espinosa Medrano published in Lima in 1662 a long defense of Góngora's poetry, *Apologético en favor de don Luis de Góngora príncipe de los poetas lyricos de España* (Apology in Favor of Don Luis de Góngora, Prince of the Lyric Poets of Spain). For his time and ours, Espinosa Medrano's essay is probably the best explanation of the power and appeal of Góngora's poetics and of Hispanic Baroque poetics in general.

In his own complex, baroque language, full of hyperbatons, or syntactic dislocations, alterations of normal word order, and wordplay of all sorts, Espinosa Medrano argues that Góngora surpassed even Latin eloquence: there is much to imitate in his excellence, much to admire in his spirit. Acknowledging that the myth of Polyphemus was narrated by Homer in the *Odyssey*, Virgil in the *Aeneid*, and Ovid in the *Metamorphoses*, "who among them," Lunarejo asks rhetorically, "achieved the eminence of the Castilian muse of Don Luis?" It seems that Góngora alone wrote the *Polyphemus*, Lunarejo continues, because only in Góngora's poem does the Cyclops burst forth, larger than life, as a true giant incarnate.

Espinosa Medrano practices his theory of poetry in his prose, whose flashes of fire (*centellas*) are not merely expression but substance. He argues that the power of poetic representation can be explained by the fact that the nature of poetry is contained and revealed in its very form, and that form is the concept in which genius or ingenuity is expressed. Therein lies the modernity of Lunarejo and the Hispanic Baroque. In a double-barreled, tour-de-force argument Lunarejo corrects Faria's assertion that Góngora's poetry should have a "poetic soul," which, as Lunarejo points out, is the term used for allegory in heroic epic poetry. This criterion is not applicable to Góngora's poetry because it is lyrical and erotic, and thus has no need for allegory. However, Lunarejo continues, if by "soul" one means the sparks of intellectual ardor that animate Góngora's divine song, then his every verse has a thousand souls, every concept a thousand splendors.

Codifying his baroque understanding of poetic language as a deviation from the patterns of everyday speech, Lunarejo argues that poetic language is a secondary product of nature's creatures. Thus hyperbaton is not an embellishment or a defect but, in fact, the "nature" or essence of the language of poetry. In this regard, Espinosa Medrano sets Gongorism apart from the Petrarchan model of poetic language elaborated in Spain by the poet Garcilaso, and he implicitly rejects the style of sixteenth-century Castilian prose writing that prized the creation of the illusion of the naturalness of everyday speech. Espinosa Medrano thus dismisses the views of Juan de Valdés in his *Diálogo de la lengua* of 1535, which had been practiced before that date by Hernán Pérez de Oliva and afterward by Francisco López de Gómara and even Bernal Díaz del Castillo. The baroque prose of Espinosa Medrano is the harbinger of the prose to follow in the works of Sor Juana Inés de la Cruz and Carlos de Sigüenza y Góngora.

Often linked with Góngora, the lyrical voice of Sor Juana Inés de la Cruz (1648–95) reigned supreme in colonial Spanish America and was extolled in the Hispanic world at large. Born in Nepantla at two days' distance from the Mexican capital, when just a girl she was brought to the viceregal court where she served five years as a lady-in-waiting; her first biographer tells how she astonished the gentlemen of the court with her mostly autodidactic learning. She spent her adult life as a Hieronymite nun who helped administer the affairs of her convent in Mexico City and supported it by writing compositions in verse commissioned by civic and church officials.

Sor Juana knew intimately the writings of the great Spanish poets of her day, and her works were published in Spain before and after her death. Her autobiographical defense of her right to study and learning, "Respuesta a Sor Filotea" ("Reply to Sister Philothea") of 1691, is simultaneously so learned and so engaging that in 1991 it inspired a feature-length film, *Yo, la peor de todas* (I, the Worst of All), directed by the Argentine filmmaker María Luisa Bemberg

Dezima Mvsa.

V. R. de la M. R. M. Juana Ynes
de la Cruz Fenix de la America,
Gloriose defempeño de fu Sexo,
Honrra de la Nacion de efte nuevo
Mundo, y argumento de las aduara-
ciones, y elogios de el Antiguo.
Nacio el dia 12. de Nov.e de el año de
1651. a las once de la Noche. Racivio
el Sagrado Habito de el Maximo D.r
S. S. Geronimo en fu Conv.to de ef.ta
Ciudad de Mexico, de edad del 2.a,s
y murio Domingo 17.de Abril de el
de 1695. de edad de 43.a, cinco me-
zes, cinco dias, y cinco horas a...s

Requiefcat inpace. Amen.

11. Sor Juana Inés de la Cruz, the "tenth muse," in a portrait by Fray Miguel de Herrera, 1732.

and based on the Mexican Nobel laureate Octavio Paz's massive, admiring literary biography of 1982, *Sor Juana Inés de la Cruz, o las trampas de la fe* (Sor Juana, or the Traps of Faith).

In her poetry Sor Juana Inés variously portrays the vicissitudes of love with longing or with irony, lambasts the follies and fickleness of men with impunity, and skewers the shortcomings of contemporary poetry, establishing her own authority even as she demurs from celebrating it. She does all this in virtuoso performances of poetic language. This is nowhere more apparent than in her hilarious poetic account of the impossibility of painting in words a perfect portrait of a classic beauty, owing to the poetic narrator's professed lack of skill as well as a larger deterrent: "Everything has already been said by the ancients!"

Sor Juana chooses here a highly demanding poetic form called the *ovillejo*, coming from the Latin *ovum*, or egg, in reference to the shape of a ball of woolen yarn. It required a technical nimbleness far exceeding the demands of the seven- and eleven-syllable poetic form known as the *silva*, in which the poet freely set verse distribution and rhyming patterns. The *ovillejo* set strict limits on such latitude, and Sor Juana's poetic narrator employs it to portray all the beauteous Lisarda's physical attributes, from her gorgeous head of hair down to her dainty feet, at which point the foot of poetic meter (*el pie de Arte Mayor*) is confounded with the young lady's foot, of which the narrator, alas! has no firsthand knowledge. The ball of yarn, *ovillejo*, is, as it were, delightfully unraveled.

In a very different register, Sor Juana's "Respuesta a Sor Filotea" combines encyclopedic knowledge of classical and biblical literature with scholastic argumentation and vivid autobiographical anecdotes. Its composition had been prompted by the bishop of Puebla, Manuel Fernández de Santa Cruz, who urged Sor Juana to write down her critique of a widely circulated sermon by the Portuguese Jesuit Antonio de Vieira. The bishop then had Sor Juana's disquisition published in 1690 under the title "Carta atenagórica" (Letter Worthy of Athena); it was accompanied by a letter, written to Sor Juana as a preface and admonishment, by the bishop under the pseudonym of Sor Philothea. To this Sor Juana replied, and her 1691 "Respuesta," published posthumously in 1700, stands today as one of the most universally read and admired prose texts of the Hispanic Baroque.

Perhaps the culmination of her work as a poet is "Primero sueño" ("First Dream"), which was published in 1692 in the first edition of volume 2 of her works. "Primero sueño" is the secular journey of the human spirit in search of knowledge of the cosmos in which the external senses are shut down and the internal senses, producing images, dreams, fantasies, and memory, are activated in sleep. Here Sor Juana effects a fully Baroque transformation of the world of nature. Mediated by references and allusions from classical mythology, nature already has been once transformed as Sor Juana cites its creatures in their (second) metamorphoses from classical divinities into earthbound animals.

Erroneously described by its first editor as a poem in imitation of Luis de Góngora, "Primero sueño" has more in common conceptually with Pedro Calderón de la Barca and his allegorical dramatized religious parables (*autos sacramentales*) of the 1630s through the 1670s, and her learned poetic vocabulary owes a considerable debt to the Renaissance poetry of Fernando de Herrera. Fascinated by the German Jesuit Athanasius Kircher's theories about the origins of human knowledge, Sor Juana creates pyramids in her poem, thus paying homage to his Egyptology as well as to Mexico's pyramids, some found in nature and others manmade by the ancient Mexicans. Although the poetic subject's ascent does not reach the ethereal realm of pure knowledge, its secular motivation and perspective subtly and earnestly complement the human soul's mystical flight to union with God represented in the writings of the Spanish mystical poets Santa Teresa de Ávila and San Juan de la Cruz.

In thematic range, linguistic virtuosity, and intellectual perspicacity, Sor Juana was rightly called, on the title page of the first edition of her works' first volume, the "unique poetess, the tenth Muse." Appearing in Madrid in 1689, the tome was titled *Inundación castálida* in reference to the fountain or sacred spring Castalia, located at the foot of Mount Parnassus dedicated to the Muses. The editor or patron who created the title, however, judged this first gathering of Sor Juana's literary output to be not a classical fountain but a baroque flood (*inundación*). From sonnets to songs to theatrical works, both sacred and profane, and even compositions in Nahuatl such as the *tocotín*, or dance song, Sor Juana's literary work was well known in her day in both Spains, old and New.

Overall, no poet of the Spanish colonial period has been translated with the frequency or fervor lavished on Sor Juana. Her editors and translators include the poet Samuel Beckett, the gifted literary translator Margaret Sayers Peden, the scholars Alan Trueblood, Electa Arenal, Kathleen Myers, Amanda Powell, Nina Scott, Mónica Díaz, and others. They all attest to the vibrant, expressive core of Sor Juana's work that transcends the concerns of her day and our own. The current interest in Sor Juana has generated studies devoted to other visionary or courageous women writers of the viceregal period, such as Catalina de Erauso, María de San José, and Úrsula Suárez. In that regard the brilliant young woman from Nepantla (meaning, appropriately, "in between") has inspired the recovery and appreciation of the works of her feminine peers and successors as whose emblem she stands here.

One of Sor Juana's intellectual companions was a man of many talents, the ex-Jesuit Carlos de Sigüenza y Góngora (1645–1700). He has been called "the archetypal Baroque gentleman," installed in the landscape that belonged to him, executor of the tasks that awaited him, and producer of all the pleasures of the intellectual life. Like Sor Juana, Sigüenza was born and died in New Spain. Unlike her, his life in a religious order was brief; he took his first vows as a Jesuit in 1662 but was expelled in 1668, punished for a nocturnal ramble undertaken after escaping the novitiates' dormitory one night. He spent nearly a decade unsuccessfully seeking readmission to the order; still, he willed his earthly goods to the Society of Jesus and was buried in a Jesuit chapel. Like Sor Juana, he had a precocious intelligence and he was engaged, often polemically, with intellectuals at home and abroad.

Though lacking in formal titles, he won the *oposiciones,* or formal competition by examination, for a position as professor of mathematics and astrology at the century-old University of Mexico. Giving evidence of his readings of Descartes, Galileo, Kepler, and Copernicus, Sigüenza strove to substitute the discipline of astronomy for astrology, as his works on the nature of comets attest and as his advocacy of scientific analysis based on empirical experimentation makes clear. He participated in geographical expeditions to chart the Gulf of Mexico coastline at the viceroy's request and, although he held the exalted title of royal cosmographer, he complained that the high-sounding honorific was far more symbolic than real.

Sigüenza reveals his interest in European global politics in his fictional narrative *Infortunios de Alonso Ramírez* (Misfortunes of Alonso Ramírez), published in 1690. Often compared to the Spanish picaresque novel, *Infortunios* also has an American antecedent in the *relación de méritos y servicios,* that is, a certified firsthand account of one's meritorious deeds and those of one's ancestors, presented to a higher authority for recognition of services rendered. *Infortunios* resonates with earlier Americanist writings. In particular, Álvar Núñez Cabeza de Vaca's *Naufragios* reveals Sigüenza's deep interest in history—a more valuable pursuit than fiction, he remarks, as he creates, precisely in fiction, the vagabond life that led his protagonist Alonso Ramírez first to Acapulco, from there to the Philippines, and ultimately around the world. As with Cabeza de Vaca, the perils of life on the high seas are grim. If in *Naufragios* French corsairs are merely threats, in *Infortunios* they are realized: Ramírez is enslaved by English pirates whose exploits drive the narrative.

Sigüenza echoes Las Casas's *Brevísima relación de la destrucción de las Indias* when, in the area that today would correspond to Vietnam, the English pirates purchase native women and briefly settle down with them before embarking for other shores, burning the native settlements and murdering the women they have left pregnant. Celebrating this victory, the English pirates quench their thirst with brandy and, after cutting off bits of the roasted arm of a human victim of the conflagration, "praised the flavor of such fine flesh and ate it up amid repeated toasts." Thus, Sigüenza ensconces the English in the place of the Spanish in this "brief account" of wanton destruction and violence. Intended or not, he performs a subtle act of literary revenge for the early English translation of Las Casas's *Brevísima relación* by Spain's British arch rivals.

As a poet who participated in the literary academies of his day and edited poetry collections, Sigüenza gladly counted Luis de Góngora among his distant forebears. Sigüenza's religious-historical poem of 1662, *Primavera Indiana* (Springtime in the Indies), pays homage to Bernardo de Balbuena's *Grandeza Mexicana*'s "Primavera inmortal" and to Mexico's popular religious culture. Its topic is the Virgin of Guadalupe, Mexico's revered patron saint. Sigüenza here reveals his passionate interest in the history and archaeology of ancient Mexico, and their relationship to contemporary New Spain. Because of that interest, Sigüenza possessed (and prized) the papers and manuscripts of Fernando de Alva Ixtlilxochitl, the Texcocan historian of ancient Mexico. The Italian scholar-traveler Giovanni Francesco Gemelli visited Sigüenza during his tour of New Spain and copied from Alva Ixtlilxochitl's papers the portrait of Moctezuma II that he later reproduced in his *Giro intorno al mondo* (Tour around the World) of 1699. The Mexican creole Jesuit Francisco Javier Clavigero would still later study the Alva Ixtlilxochitl/Sigüenza collection and reproduce its portrait of Moctezuma in his ancient history of Mexico, *Storia antica di Messico*.

Of greatest interest today is Sigüenza's *Teatro de virtudes políticas que constituyen a un príncipe* (Spectacle or Display of Civic Virtues that Constitute a Prince) of 1680. The treatise accompanied a triumphal arch that Sigüenza designed for the processional entry into the city of New Spain's new viceroy, Tomás Antonio de la Cerda, Marqués de la Laguna. (This civic ritual had been observed since the arrival of the first judges of the high court of New Spain, or *Audiencia Real*, in 1528.) Sor Juana participated by designing the triumphal arch for the cathedral, choosing the theme of the pagan god Neptune to celebrate the viceroy's virtues by paying homage to the aquatic references in his noble title, "laguna," or lagoon, as well as to the island city, Mexico Tenochtitlan, where he would rule. Sigüenza received the commission for the church of Santo Domingo, and he chose as his theme the Aztec dynasty of pre-Columbian Mexico.

A truly synthetic work, *Teatro* was inspired by the tradition of the education of Christian princes, the Jesuit inclination to honor earlier cultural traditions, and Sigüenza's own creole patriotism, projecting for New Spain a noble past and a brilliant future. Sigüenza follows Athanasius Kircher's *Oedipus Aegyptiacus* (Egyptian Oedipus) of 1652–54, which reconciled esoteric philosophical speculation with empirical research, to demonstrate that Catholic doctrine was the fulfillment of humanity's spiritual quest. In taking up Kircher, Sigüenza makes the claim that the ancient Mexicans descended from Naphtuhim, the founder and ruler of ancient Egypt who was the son of Misraim (or Egypt), who was the son of Ham and grandson of Noah, thus making Egypt the origin of all natural wisdom and religion and Mexico its ultimate heir.

Sigüenza brings together the Renaissance tradition of *empresas*, symbolic representations containing esoteric signs that were the patrimony of a single individual or family, with the iconographic symbols associated with the Aztec rulers. The descriptions in his *Teatro* thus make legible to the Western eye the emblems of the native lords found in colonial Mexican codices, such as the one, now housed at the John Carter Brown Library in Providence, Rhode Island, commissioned by the Jesuit Juan de Tovar circa 1585 and studied by his colleague José de Acosta.

12. Acamapich, the first Aztec king of Mexico, holding the green reeds that represent his name, identified with the Christian virtue of hope by Carlos de Sigüenza y Góngora.

Sigüenza praises this first king of the Aztecs, Acamapich, for creating a sovereign regime when elected in 1361 and for liberating his people from the "violent tyranny" of the Tepanecas and Acolhuas (the latter were Fernando de Alva Ixtlilxochitl's forebears). The meaning of the name "Acamapich" is "a hand holding many reeds," which is also the king's iconographic symbol; Sigüenza ascribes to it the Christian virtue of hope. Citing authorities from Genesis to Lucan, he writes an octave of eleven-syllable verses in which the green reeds, the "brilliant jewel" in the king's hand, become the "rustic scepter" that exceeds the beauty of palms and which sprouts forth the laurel branch. Tovar's pictorial representation and Sigüenza's processional commemoration draw together the Aztec and Christian cultural traditions, asserting respect for both but the priority of one. These syncretic moves recall the Nahua/Franciscan colloquies, recorded in 1564 by Fray Bernardino

Sahagún and his Nahua collaborators, that depict the reign of the ancient Aztec law and its loss.

Sigüenza's grafting of ancient Mexican tradition to the New Spain of his era does not stop there. He is the first Mexican thinker to identify the legendary Mexican man-god Quetzalcoatl as Saint Thomas. Earlier writers on ancient Peru had cautiously postulated apostolic visits, associating them with pre-Columbian legend, such as El Inca Garcilaso's and Guaman Poma's speculations about a visit from Saint Bartholomew to the Andes. More boldly, Sigüenza directly matches Saint Thomas with one of the most revered lords of ancient Mexican mythology. This legacy would be given new life in the following century.

Chapter 9
On to independence

In the late eighteenth century there emerged a new "polemics of possession" occasioned by the drive for Latin American independence. Literary and cultural initiatives were central to its purpose. Although the Spanish-born colonial official Alonso Carrió de la Vandera and the Mexican Jesuit historian Francisco Javier Clavigero did not advocate for independence, their writings nevertheless laid important cultural groundwork for it by looking, respectively, down the long roads of the South American continent and deep into the past. They would come to be considered as uniquely American and therefore crucial to the cause. Subsequently, the Mexican Dominican friar Servando Teresa de Mier and the Venezuelan-born scholar, poet, and educator Andrés Bello labored for independence from abroad and came back from exile to take their places in an independent Latin America. Carrió de la Vandera and Clavigero anticipate the end of the Spanish colonial period; Mier and Bello transcend the achievement of independence and set the tone for the literary cultural work that, in Latin America, would continue to be engaged with the cultural politics and the political life of the new republics.

El Lazarillo de ciegos caminantes (A Guide for Blind Travelers) was written under a thinly disguised pseudonym: Don Calixto Bustamante Carlos Inca, alias Concolorcorvo, "a native of Cuzco," the former Inca capital. Although the title page announced the site of publication as Gijón, Asturias, Spain, in 1773, with royal license, it was actually published in Lima, in 1775 or 1776, without official authorization. It was authored by Alonso Carrió de la Vandera (ca. 1715–83), who had spent a half century in America serving the Spanish crown, and its title alludes to the inaugural Spanish picaresque novel, *El Lazarillo de Tormes*, published anonymously in 1554. Like its namesake, the South American *Lazarillo* serves as a guide, in this case for continent-spanning wayfarers rather than for urban Castilian masters, but its thrust is likewise satirical. The name "Concolorcorvo" (*con color corvo*, of dark color) is taken from a ballad by Francisco de Quevedo, "Boda de negros" (Blacks' Wedding), and Carrió de la Vandera refers to "the great Quevedo" as he cites his verses.

Setting the scene as the long trek over the rough-and-tumble highways and byways of the viceroyalties from Buenos Aires to Lima, Carrió de la Vandera parodies and dismantles late seventeenth- and eighteenth-century travel literature devoted to the Americas that was rife with distortions and falsehoods. In the voice of his "pure Indian" (*indio neto*) narrator and assistant Calixto, Carrió satirizes the debates on the origins of the New World's natives. The clandestine character of *Lazarillo*'s origin and its contents are aimed at attacking the author's enemies with whom he was engaged in a polemic about the deleterious effects of contraband trade. *Lazarillo* is an encoded text that demands that its readers understand the dissimulation and comprehend the origin of corruption in the viceroyalty: a contraband operation that carried illegal goods from Guatemala to the kingdom of Quito and southward to Lima, Chile, Buenos Aires, and Montevideo. The objects of Carrió de la Vandera's satire are colonial officials of the highest level—viceroys, bishops and archbishops, presidents and judges of the *Real Audiencia*, or high court—whom he scorns for their tacit approval of, and participation in, economic corruption.

Carrió de la Vandera's literary language is characterized by Quevedesque crispness, proverbs and sayings, indigenous Amerindian words and expressions, Latin terms and phrases, classical citations, and Gallicisms. Well versed in the chronicles of the conquest of the Indies as well as Spanish narrative and poetic literature, Carrió de la Vandera takes as his most revered model the Spanish Benedictine monk Benito Jerónimo Feijóo, "lover of the natural sciences, devotee of the critical spirit, and of the most alert attention to reality."

Like Juan del Valle y Caviedes, Carrió de la Vandera is strongly critical of creoles' ignorance of their world in all its dimensions. His foil is a gentleman traveler from Tucumán (in today's Argentina) carrying with him four books, all of which are useless for understanding America: the fictional travel book of the Portuguese explorer and writer Fernão Mendes Pinto about journeys to Africa and Asia, a treatise on the pagan gods of antiquity, a romance of chivalry, and a book about the civil wars between the Abencerrajes and the Zegrís, rival Moorish houses in late medieval Granada. Regarding his own American homeland, Carrió de la Vandera laments, the traveler knows nothing; he can speak only about his local district, and all his accounts are so mixed up and garbled that they seem to be the "delirium or dreams of waking men."

In *Lazarillo* no group, no caste, no class is exempt from being satirized, and foreigners also fall victim to the author's pen. Those *monsiures*, or rather "m'lords" or distinguished French, English, or Italian gentlemen, our narrator insists, think only to knock down the Spaniards, publishing first in their pamphlets and then in their general histories all manner of anti-Spanish lies (the Black Legend at work). He argues that the Indians should be allowed to learn to speak Spanish, but priests' assistants stand in the way, condemning Spanish-speaking natives as pretentious and pseudo-learned for relentlessly pursuing justice. (This echoes Guaman Poma's complaints of a century and a half earlier of being called a "busybody, *ladino* jerk" for the same reasons.)

Carrió de la Vandera defends the merits and talents of the creoles, which he considers to be as excellent as those of Spaniards. When in one of his anecdotes an old man celebrates the virtues of Spain and vituperates those of Peru, his great-grandson replies that the only thing left is to claim that the Eucharist consecrated in Spain is superior to that of the Indies. The old man retorts, "Of course it is, because they're made of better flour!" A truly scandalous reply it would have been, our narrator comments, if it had not been taken in the jocose spirit with which the old man intended to put his great-grandson in his place.

In short, *Lazarillo* guides the reader through the geographical length and breadth and the immoral depths of viceregal society in all their variety. With bold Quevedesque humor its narrator lays bare all local faults, as well as those of the larger community of humankind. Far from being a narrowly focused lampoon of the representation of native contempt and self-hatred, the clandestinely published *Lazarillo de ciegos caminantes* exposes the failings of Spanish colonial governance and the frailties of humanity itself. This is the merit that Carrió de la Vandera perceived in Quevedo's works and for this reason he calls the Spanish poet and thinker "the great."

The second half of the eighteenth century brought the tumult of the expulsion of the Jesuit Order from all Spanish territories in 1767; in 1773 the Society of Jesus was suppressed altogether by Pope Clement XIV as a result of controversies over its political and economic maneuverings. Thus exiled from his homeland to Italy, the Mexican creole Jesuit Francisco Javier Clavigero (1731–87) wrote his *Historia antigua de México* (History of Ancient Mexico), which he translated into Italian as *Storia antica di Messico*, published in 1780–81. It soon appeared in English and

German, and its renown was such that it was read and cited by Thomas Jefferson and Edward Gibbon, among others.

Born in Veracruz to prominent Spanish parents, Clavigero took his Jesuit novitiate in 1748–50 north of the viceregal capital at the Jesuit church and seminary in Tepotzotlan, established in 1582 and maintained until the expulsion. Clavigero likely began his study of Nahuatl there, but he would perfect his knowledge of the language (and eventually write a grammar of it) at the Colegio de San Gregorio in Mexico City and at the Colegio de San Francisco Javier in Puebla. Subsequently assigned to *colegios* for Jesuits in New Spain's Valladolid and Guadalajara, upon expulsion Clavigero was sent to Bologna, where he lived from 1769 until his death in 1787, working as a diocesan priest under the jurisdiction of the local bishop. In Bologna Clavigero grew Mexican plants and wrote his immensely successful, polemical history of ancient Mexico. With the focused passion and nostalgic determination of the exile, he aspired to recover his lost homeland and defend it from the influential European philosophers who theorized that America and all that inhabited it suffered a natural inferiority.

Clavigero's history of ancient Mexico relies heavily on Fray Juan de Torquemada's *Monarquía Indiana*, published in 1615 and frequently cited as the culmination of Franciscan scholarship on New Spain. Clavigero's merit was to turn its baroque prose into a direct and swift narration. His accounts of the natural world and native civilizations of Mexico are followed by a volume of ancillary dissertations; these refute the views on America of the Dutch-born Prussian philologist and historian Cornelius de Pauw with regard to human conduct, those of the Comte de Buffon Georges-Louis Leclerc on the animal world, and the works of the Abbé Guillaume-Thomas-François Raynal and William Robertson on the history of ancient Mexico.

Clavigero's true vocation was pedagogical. If it was impossible for him to exercise his teaching vocation in Bologna as he had in the

Jesuit *colegios* and Indian schools of Mexico, he could do so now only through his writing. In his history, his reliance on the visual medium of communication best reveals his deepest convictions and achievement. The copper engravings that complement the prose narration of the *Storia antica di Messico* emphasize the historical value of ancient Mexican painting and are central to the work's purpose. Clavigero directed the production of some twenty engravings for the first edition of 1780–81, which in turn were carefully copied and reproduced in all editions of his work up to 1945, when Clavigero's original Spanish-language manuscript was published for the first time.

The models for some of the engravings were early colonial Mexican manuscripts. Others were Americanist works already in print, such as Giovanni Francesco Gemelli's *Giro intorno al mondo*. Gemelli had relied on Carlos de Sigüenza y Góngora's collection of Fernando de Alva Ixtlilxochitl's Mexican paintings; Clavigero studied them in Mexico in 1759. The Jesuit historian advises the reader that the engravings will facilitate the understanding of unfamiliar topics such as the Mexican calendar system and the institutions of ancient ritual life and its architecture. He also insists that his illustrations serve to correct the "lying, engraved images and figures" found in works by Theodore de Bry, Thomas Gage, and Pieter van der Aa. Van der Aa's work, for example, depicted ancient ambassadors arriving at the Aztec court in Mexico Tenochtitlan mounted on elephants. "These are very great lies indeed!" harangues an indignant Clavigero.

One of his engravings sums up his outlook on ancient history and his program for the future. Three young women make maize bread: one sifts the kernels of corn, another prepares them on the grinding stone, or *metate*, and the third molds the dough for cooking on the griddle, or *comal*, over an open fire. The model for this composition is found in Girolamo Benzoni's *Historia del Mondo Nuovo* (History of the New World), published in 1565. The carefully disheveled hair (lice-infected, Benzoni wrote) of these three young women of strong limbs and natural grace signifies the barbaric past and the hard life presently endured. Unique in Clavigero's engraving is the steady gaze of one of the young women, who looks out at the viewer with curiosity—or defiance. This reading is suggested by Clavigero's comments on the colonial oppression and poverty suffered by the Mexican Indian nations in spite of the prudent laws promulgated by the Spanish monarchs. "A deadly example," Clavigero writes, "of Divine Justice and the instability of the world's kingdoms." The young woman's gaze reiterates the doubt registered verbally in the colloquy between Aztec priests and Franciscan friars written down by Fray Bernardino de Sahagún and his Nahua colleagues in the 1560s: "Are we to give up our ancient law?" The eyes of this defiant young Mexican woman ask, "And what are we to give up now?"

Modo di fare il pane.
1 Donna che pela il grano. 2 che il macina. 3 che forma e cuoce il pane.

13. Francisco Javier Clavigero's depiction of the process of making bread from maize, "the seed that Providence gave to the Indies."

If the young woman's gesture is accusatory, the pictorial ensemble is nevertheless positive in meaning on two levels: working together in harmony and peace, these young women dramatize Clavigero's main thesis about converting nature into culture, or rather, employing the former in the service of the latter. In this display of "the raw and the cooked," the maize-bread-making tableau reiterates the principle of nature put to culture's use as visualized more than two centuries earlier in Oviedo's *Historia general* drawing of the Taíno hammock. Clavigero describes maize as "that seed that Providence bequeathed to that part of the world," suggesting that it might well be the truest gold of the Indies, not simply capable of defending the merits of a lost past but also of sustaining and advancing contemporary society and civilization.

One of Clavigero's devoted readers, Fray Servando Teresa de Mier (1763–1827), also looked ahead. He anticipated Mexican independence by looking back, that is, by bending to his purposes major writings and events in colonial Spanish American history and thought. His signal achievement was his *Historia de la revolución de la Nueva España* (History of the Revolution of New Spain), published in London in 1813 under the pseudonym José Guerra. He also wrote a series of public letters on the popular tradition of the Virgin of Guadalupe and the need for political independence, published in the period from 1797 to 1820.

Fray Servando is best remembered for the sermon he preached on December 12, 1794, at the Collegiate Church of Guadalupe, in Mexico City, in which he presented the thesis that the Spaniards had not brought the Christian gospel to Mexico but rather that Saint Thomas had done so a millennium and a half earlier in an apostolic visit to the Indies. Furthermore, he declared, the venerated image of the Virgin of Guadalupe had not been impressed in 1531 on the cape of the Indian Juan Diego (Juan Diego Cuauhtlatoatzin was canonized as a saint by Pope John Paul II in 2002), but rather on the garment of Saint Thomas himself.

Thus Fray Servando took up the proposal that Carlos de Sigüenza y Góngora had made in a now-lost work of the 1690s. Although Sigüenza and others had suffered no personal consequence for their speculations, Fray Servando was immediately sequestered and his authorization to preach revoked.

Sentenced soon afterward to ten years' imprisonment, Fray Servando began a peripatetic existence, in and out of jail, in Europe, the Caribbean, the United States, and Mexico. He spent the last decade of his life in post-independence Mexico, participating in Mexico's Second Constituent Congress and signing the Constitutive Act of Federation. Assigned an annual pension and living quarters in Mexico's National Palace, he died in 1827 and was interred in the monastery of Santo Domingo in Mexico City. In 1861 his corpse was sold to a circus owner and it is said to have been exhibited in Europe in 1882. In death as in life, Fray Servando's fate was so colorful and outrageous that his memoirs, his *Apología* of 1818, inspired the Cuban author Reinaldo Arenas in 1965 to write his breathtaking novel *El mundo alucinante* (The Hallucinating World), which was first published in 1969.

Fray Servando's literary career was a starburst exploding in all directions; he reviewed and commented on the writings of Bartolomé de Las Casas, Fray Gregorio García, José de Acosta, and Clavigero, among others, and he had dealings with major figures of his day, particularly during his time in London from 1811 to 1816. These associations included the Spanish liberal exile José Blanco White, Simón Bolívar's tutor Simón Rodríguez, Bolívar himself, and Andrés Bello. Fray Servando maintained a long friendship with Blanco White. In 1811–12 they debated whether the Spanish viceroyalties in America were ready for independence: Blanco said no, Fray Servando yes; both ultimately advocated its cause. In 1812 Fray Servando prologized and published editions of Las Casas's 1552 *Brevísima relación de la destrucción de las Indias* in London,

Philadelphia, Mexico City, Guadalajara, Bogotá, and possibly in Cádiz, Spain.

In his historical and polemical writings, Fray Servando subscribed to Las Casas's fundamental ideas: first, the Indians had never offended the Spanish, who therefore had no right to make war against them; second, the papal bulls of donation of 1493, granting Castile sovereignty over the lands Columbus might discover (modified in 1494 by the Treaty of Tordesillas dividing the unknown lands between Spain and Portugal), authorized only the right to evangelize but not to conquer; third, the infamous Requerimiento (Requirement), the formal ultimatum to be read (in Spanish) to newly encountered Indians, offering them the alternatives of immediate submission or war to the death, deserved the harshest ridicule and condemnation. Also like Las Casas, Fray Servando rejected the attribution of satanic origin to Amerindian religions: the human desire for knowledge of the Creator was a natural phenomenon, and idolatry, a perversion of the natural order, was caused simply by human ignorance and error. Fray Servando maintained his belief in the apostolic mission and therefore the spiritual independence of Mexico which, as political independence neared, met with an increasingly enthusiastic reception.

Fray Servando had a probing and intimate knowledge of the writers on America who preceded him. He criticized José de Acosta for identifying the origin of native Mexican religion as the work of Satan, suggesting that the Jesuit had followed his confrere Juan de Tovar's account too closely. Fray Servando argued that all missionaries, right up to the present day, had failed to perceive or point out the clear vestiges of Christian ritual and belief found among America's most primitive and ancient peoples. Fray Servando cited as authoritative the views of the friars Gregorio García, Antonio Calancha, Alonso Ramos Gavilán, and the ex-Jesuit Sigüenza y Góngora on apostolic visits to America as well as Clavigero on the dignity and merit of ancient Mexican culture. In "Nota Undécima de la Segunda Carta de un Americano" (The Eleventh Note of the Second Letter of an American) of 1812 Fray Servando condemned the "great calumny against America," that is, the theory about its natural inferiority, citing De Pauw as the author who did the greatest harm because his views were communicated in the meetings of the Spanish legislature (*Cortes*) in Cádiz.

In his *Historia* Fray Servando makes Las Casas the father of the creoles of New Spain as well as the protector of the Indians. He resolves this contradictory position regarding the creoles as the descendants of cruel and greedy conquistadores by fancifully asserting that the New Laws of 1542 had not been revoked but in fact were honored, thus protecting the Indians and preventing further conquests. By this sleight of hand Fray Servando turns the creoles into the spiritual heirs of the mendicant friars who had defended the Indians in the sixteenth century. But, unlike Las Casas, Fray Servando in his era fought not for the redemption of humanity but for the liberation of the Mexican nation. Fray Servando has been cited as being the principal theorist of the Mexican movement for independence from Spain.

In a similar spirit, Simón Bolívar called upon Las Casas's views in his assessment of Latin America's independence struggles and prospects for its future as outlined in his *Carta de Jamaica* (Letter from Jamaica) of September 6, 1815. He cites Las Casas's *Brevísima relación de la destrucción de las Indias* as a work founded on the authority of authentic documents and warranted by the most respected sources. In these claims Bolívar follows Fray Servando's *Historia* almost to the letter, including his praise for Las Casas as "the philanthropic bishop of Chiapas, apostle of America,... friend of humanity." In November 1821, Andrés Bello wrote from London to Fray Servando in Philadelphia, reporting that "the latest news from Mexico [regarding the agitation for independence] has caused quite a sensation" and suggesting that "monarchy (limited, of course) is the only government suitable for us."

Having in hand Fray Servando's *Historia* of 1813, Bello urged the Dominican to write a "complete history of the Mexican revolution," leaving out "certain rhetorical passages that are not compatible with the impartiality of history." He argued that it was sufficient to do no more than preserve the memory of events because "that alone is enough to heap the enemies of our cause with infamy." Bello admonished Fray Servando to keep in mind that he was writing for posterity, not just for the journalists of his day, adding, while professing his inalterable friendship, "I am afraid that I am a voice crying in the wilderness, and that your blood is too hot to follow this advice."

Of cooler temperament, Andrés Bello (1781–1865) was one of the most influential figures of Latin American literary and intellectual life in the nineteenth century. He was the consummate, independence-era Janus, looking penetratingly back and soberly forward. Born in Caracas, at age twenty he assisted the German naturalist and explorer Alexander von Humboldt in his Venezuelan researches and accompanied him on the ascent of Mount Ávila. At thirty Bello joined Simón Bolívar in London to seek, unsuccessfully, the British government's recognition of the Americanist cause and to serve as Bolívar's tutor and secretary. Bello resided in London from 1810 to 1829.

In the library of the British Museum Bello studied classical and medieval philology, revised a Spanish translation of the Bible, edited the manuscripts of British philosopher Jeremy Bentham, and produced an erudite, authoritative edition of the twelfth-century Castilian *Poema del Mío Cid* (Poem of the Cid). He also wrote a grammar of the Castilian language for his fellow Latin Americans, *Gramática de la lengua castellana destinada al uso de los americanos*, that would be published in 1847. Because of his contact with English and French Romantics in London, and his translation of Lord Byron, Alphonse de Lamartine, and Victor Hugo while in Chile, he stood at the cusp of Romanticism in Spanish America, where he introduced the European Romantic notion of literature as the product of the fusion of human consciousness with the natural environment; in this organic and biological model, culture emerges from natural origins rooted in history and geography.

Bello was well aware that he was participating in the task of shaping the cultural dimensions of the newly independent republics and that the way to foment cultural unity and stability among them was to connect the emerging nations, through the written word, "to a common nature, a common land, the pre-Columbian land that had always been there." In London in 1823 he published the two-volume *La Biblioteca Americana, o Miscelánea de literatura, artes i ciencias* (The American Library, or Miscellany of Literature, the Arts, and Sciences) and, in 1826, the *Repertorio Americano* (American Repertory), of which he was principal author and editor.

Bello described the *Biblioteca*'s purpose as announcing new advances in technology, "making sure to germinate the fertile seed of liberty," establishing the basis for teaching morality and preserving the deeds of history, all of which he considered to be "the noble, vast, and difficult task that the love of homeland has placed upon us." Devoted to the natural and physical sciences and the humanities, the *Biblioteca* and *Repertorio* had as their stated goal to give "preference to everything related to America, especially the productions of America's children, and to its history. . . . Through original essays and historical documents, we propose to illustrate some of the most interesting events of our revolution, unknown to much of the world and even to Americans themselves."

Bello's "Alocución a la poesía" (An Address to Poetry) of 1823 and his "Oda a la agricultura de la zona tórrida" (Ode to the

Agriculture of the Torrid Zone) of 1826 cast in verse some of these principles, particularly with regard to nature, the world, and the cosmos. He beckoned the allegorical figure Poetry and the other arts to leave tired Europe and come to virginal America to celebrate the "riches of all other climes" that grow and flourish here:

> Spreading your diaphanous wings,
> over the vast Atlantic go,
> to other heavens, other folk, another world,
> where earth still wears its ancient dress,
> and man has scarcely conquered it.

"Other folk, another world" echoes the cosmological and geographical themes about America heard since the days of Pietro Martire and on through those of José de Acosta. Bello's "Oda a la agricultura de la zona tórrida" expresses similar sentiments:

> Hail, fertile zone, that circumscribes
> the errant course of your enamored sun,
> and, caressed by its light,
> brings forth all living things
> in each of your many climes.

The cosmological image created by these verses, with the pointedly Copernican sun casting love and light to illuminate America's geographical grandeur, no longer lost in the shadows of ignorance, is an ode to knowledge. Bello embraces here the entire American natural historical tradition, dating from Oviedo in the early sixteenth century, as well as the long historical tradition of America, from its pre-Columbian myths to its nineteenth-century wars of liberation. All this Bello takes as preface to the great American saga of human history yet to be realized.

Bello understood the newness of America; he fulfilled some of Bolívar's stated ambitions in his "Carta de Jamaica" regarding the need for knowledge about America and for taking the measure of its worth. Bello brought forth modernity in the midst of a society that was not so. His organic theory of human culture and language, with nature and humanity working together—an achievement so admired by Oviedo in the Taínos' harnessing of nature—was modern. In this, Bello was a Romantic. Yet his neoclassical tendencies had to do precisely with the future that he postulated for America. It needed its own poet, an American Virgil; it needed to establish its own classical time; it needed to be joined by the common bond of an expressive, flexible, yet unified language. In this conviction Bello was more neoclassical than Romantic. America's greatness was yet to be realized; sung in the spirit of Virgil's *Georgics*, the utilization of nature to serve humanity's needs was the route to that achievement.

Regarding the forces of innovation and tradition in American versions of the Spanish language, Bello was engaged by his younger contemporary the Argentine Domingo Faustino Sarmiento in a polemic, carried out in print, that spanned the years 1842–44. While both opposed the rigid stagnation of the language, Sarmiento argued that the citizenry should be its arbiter, not the grammarians, whom he considered to be "like the conservative senate." Continuing the analogy between language and civil governance, Bello declared that "in language, as in politics, it is indispensible that there be a body of wise individuals that dictates the laws appropriate to language's needs."

The public polemic degenerated into a personal controversy between these two strong personalities, and in 1843 Sarmiento proposed an orthographic reform, based on American pronunciation, that would reduce the Spanish alphabet to twenty-three letters, omitting superfluous letters, such as v and z, because their sounds are represented by other letters (b, s) or because they are not pronounced, such as h. Bello opposed it but nevertheless charged a university commission to study the proposal. In 1844 the commission declared itself in favor of

Sarmiento's ideas, but Bello and others favored modifying American Spanish orthography in stages. The reform was partially adopted by the government of Chile and influenced, for a time, other Latin American republics. Bello acknowledged Sarmiento's efforts in educating the new nations in the pages of the newspaper *El Araucano*; Sarmiento in turn praised Bello, the founding president of the University of Chile. Although radical change did not occur, the principles of linguistic reform triumphed with the support of both. Debates on American Spanish would continue to engage writers, grammarians, and linguists well beyond the Bello-Sarmiento encounters. When in 1847 Bello published the *Gramática* he had written two decades earlier, it was heralded as the "first great body of grammatical doctrine of the Castilian language." Guided by the principle that grammatical facts should be understood and explained by their grammatical function rather than by their correspondence to objective values, that is, their meaning in the world of things, Bello's views took their place among the most advanced grammatical currents of his time. His efforts to "de-Latinize" Spanish were also important. In this, he celebrated the vernacular ("each language has its own theory, its own grammar"), just as Pérez de Oliva, Oviedo, Gómara, and all the other greatest writers of colonial Latin America had done in their day.

If in 1492 Antonio de Nebrija's grammar had anticipated unknowingly the spread of the Castilian language over two continents and the "islands of the Ocean Sea," the vigorous debates about Latin American Spanish in the 1840s between Bello and Sarmiento and Bello's 1847 Spanish grammar for American use constitute a fitting, nearly teleological conclusion to the three-centuries-long history of colonial Latin American literature in Spanish. Over the centuries the language's excellence was honed in historical prose and legal treatises, in poetry both epic and lyric, in fictional narrations and romance, in essays, and dramatic and comedic entertainments. Learned language was augmented by the language of the street, with the argots of particular groups in particular places finding their way into poetry, too. Midway through the colonial period, Espinosa Medrano rationalized the connection between the mundane and the sublime, and poets such as Sor Juana and Valle y Caviedes made it happen.

These innovations were not limited to native Spanish speakers of European stock. Writers of native Amerindian heritage such as Guaman Poma and Alva Ixtlilxochitl achieved unforgettable rhetorical expressiveness in the manipulation of Castilian, if not its mastery. If there was one overarching phenomenon shared by the myriad minds that created the cacophonous colonial symphony of three centuries, it was the toil and joy of seeing the Spanish language establish itself in the New World, adding prestige to its honored place in the Old.

The Spanish language was both vehicle and object of the colonial centuries' greatest polemics, but it was more than a medium or a tool. To colonial-era writers—Spanish, creole, or of Amerindian heritage—it was their claim to a place in the world they expanded and with it, the Spanish language itself. It was capacious enough to accommodate, however imperfectly, all that was new to Castilians in the New World and all that was already familiar to its ancestrally rooted inhabitants, but now in a new language. Despite the fall of empire as the Spanish knew it, this enduring, malleable vernacular nevertheless sprang with new life, phoenix-like, into a future that the learned Nebrija could not have envisioned but that, as the humanist he was, he would have applauded.

References

Introduction

José María Torres Caicedo is quoted in Arturo Ardao, *Génesis de la idea y el nombre de América Latina* (Caracas: Consejo Nacional de la Cultura, 1980), 73–74.

Thomas Jefferson, "To Thomas Mann Randolph, Jr.," in *The Papers of Thomas Jefferson*, vol. 11, *1 January to 6 August 1787*, ed. Julian P. Boyd (Princeton, NJ: Princeton University Press, 1955), 558.

Mariano Picón-Salas, *De la conquista a la Independencia: tres siglos de historia cultural hispanoamericana* (México: Fondo de Cultura Económica, 1969), 12.

Eugenio Asensio, "La lengua compañera del imperio," *Revista de Filología Española* 43 (1960):406–7.

Hernán Pérez de Oliva, "Razonamiento sobre la navegación del Guadalquivir," in *Diálogo de la dignidad del hombre. Razonamientos. Ejercicios*, ed. María Luisa Cerrón Puga (Madrid: Cátedra, 1995), 195.

Rolena Adorno, "Cultures in Contact: Mesoamerica, the Andes and the European Written Tradition," in *The Cambridge History of Latin American Literature*, ed. Roberto González Echevarría and Enrique Pupo-Walker (Cambridge: Cambridge University Press, 1996), 35, 39.

Chapter 1

Edmundo O'Gorman, "Pedro Mártir y el proceso de América," in *Cuatro historiadores de Indias: siglo XVI* (México: Secretaría de Educación Pública, 1979), 23–24.

Pietro Martire d'Anghiera, *Décadas del Nuevo Mundo*, ed. Edmundo
O'Gorman, trans. Agustín Millares Carlo, 2 vols. (Santo Domingo:
Sociedad Dominicana de Bibliófilos, 1989), 1:154 [dec. 1, bk. 5].

Hernán Pérez de Oliva, *Diálogo de la dignidad del hombre*, ed. María
Luisa Cerrón Puga (Madrid: Editora Nacional, 1982), 95–96.

Hernán Pérez de Oliva, *Historia de la Invención de las Yndias*, ed.
José Juan Arrom (Bogotá: Instituto Caro y Cuervo, 1965), 104
[octava narración], 47 [primera narración].

J. Jorge Klor de Alva, trans., "The Aztec-Spanish Dialogues (1524),"
Alcheringa 4, no. 2 (1980): 107–8, 109–10, 112–13. English
translation of the Nahuatl text of the *Libro de los coloquios* (Book
of the Colloquies).

Chapter 2

Bartolomé de las Casas, *Historia de las Indias*, ed. Agustín Millares
Carlo, estudio preliminar de Lewis Hanke, 3 vols. (México: Fondo
de Cultura Económica, 1951), 3:179 [bk. 3, chap. 102]).

Chapter 3

Juan Ginés de Sepúlveda, *Demócrates segundo o las justas causas de la
guerra contra los indios*, ed. and trans. Ángel Losada (Madrid:
Consejo Superior de Investigaciones Científicas, 1984), 21.

Juan Ginés de Sepúlveda, "Apología de Juan Ginés de Sepúlveda,"
in *Apología de Juan Ginés de Sepúlveda contra fray Bartolomé de
las Casas y de fray Bartolomé de las Casas contra Juan Ginés de
Sepúlveda*, ed. and trans. Ángel Losada (Madrid: Editora Nacional,
1975), 78.

Bartolomé de las Casas, "Apología de fray Bartolomé de las Casas,"
in Losada, *Apología de Juan Ginés de Sepúlveda*, 134, 139.

Chapter 4

Charles Gibson, "Reconquista and conquista," in *Homage to Irving
A. Leonard*, ed. Raquel Chang-Rodríguez and Donald A. Yates
(East Lansing: Latin American Studies Center, Michigan State
University, 1977), 20–21.

Anthony Pagden, "'Con título y con no menos mérito que el de
Alemania, que vuestra sacra majestad posee': Rethinking the

Conquest of Mexico," in *The Uncertainties of Empire: Essays in Iberian and Spanish-American Intellectual History* (London: Variorum, 1994), 7, 13.

Robert Lewis, "Retórica y verdad: los cargos de Bernal Díaz a López de Gómara," in *De la crónica a la nueva narrativa mexicana*, ed. Merlin H. Forster and Julio Ortega (México: Oasis, 1986), 41–43.

Cristián Roa-de-la-Carrera, *Histories of Infamy: Francisco López de Gómara and the Ethics of Spanish Imperialism* (Boulder: University Press of Colorado, 2005), 196.

Cristián Roa-de-la-Carrera, "Francisco López de Gómara and *La conquista de México*," in *Chimalpahin's Conquest: A Nahua Historian's Rewriting of Francisco López de Gómara's* La conquista de México, by Domingo Francisco de San Antón Muñón Chimalpahin Cuauhtlehuanitzin, ed. and trans. Susan Schroeder, Anne J. Cruz, Cristián Roa-de-la-Carrera, and David E. Tavárez (Stanford, CA: Stanford University Press, 2010), 43.

Bernal Díaz del Castillo, *The History of the Conquest of New Spain*, ed. Davíd Carrasco, trans. A. P. Maudslay (Albuquerque: University of New Mexico Press, 2008), 156.

Bernal Díaz del Castillo, *Historia verdadera de la conquista de la Nueva España*, ed. Joaquín Ramírez Cabañas, 2 vols. (México: Editorial Porrúa, 1977), 1:39, 1:244, 1:260, 2:365, 2:378.

Fernando de Alva Ixtlilxochitl, *Historia de la nación chichimeca*, in *Obras históricas de Fernando de Alva Ixtlilxochitl*, ed. Edmundo O'Gorman, 2 vols. (México: Universidad Nacional Autónoma de México, 1985), 2:27, 2:154, 2:194, 2:223–24, 2:259.

Fernando de Alva Ixtlilxochitl, *Sumaria relación de todas las cosas...en la Nueva España*, in *Obras históricas de Fernando de Alva Ixtlilxochitl*, 1:288.

Chapter 5

Álvar Núñez Cabeza de Vaca, *The Narrative of Cabeza de Vaca*, ed. and trans. Rolena Adorno and Patrick Charles Pautz (Lincoln: University of Nebraska Press, 2003), 46, 172.

Abel Posse, *El largo atardecer del caminante* (Buenos Aires: Emecé, 1992), 35.

Jorge Luis Borges, "The Ethnographer," in *Collected Fictions*, trans. Andrew Hurley (New York: Viking Press, 1998), 335.

Chapter 6

David Quint, "Epics of the Defeated: The Other Tradition of Lucan, Ercilla, and d'Aubigné," in *Epic and Empire: Politics and Generic Form from Virgil to Milton* (Princeton, NJ: Princeton University Press, 1993), 182–84.

Edmundo O'Gorman, "Prólogo," in *Historia natural y moral de las Indias*, by José de Acosta, ed. Edmundo O'Gorman, 2nd ed. (México: Fondo de Cultura Económica, 1962), xliii, xlix–liii.

José de Acosta, *The Natural and Moral History of the Indies*, trans. Edward Grimston, ed. Clements R. Markham, 2 vols. (New York: Burt Franklin, n.d.), 1:xxv, 2:391.

Samuel Purchas, *Hakluytus Posthumus or Purchas His Pilgrimes*, 20 vols. (Glasgow: James MacLehose and Sons, 1906), 15:233 [pt. 2, bk. 5, chap. 4], 17:412 [pt. 2, bk. 7, chap. 14].

Chapter 7

Eugenio D'Ors, *Lo barroco*, 1935, prol. Alfonso E. Pérez Sánchez, ed. Ángel D'Ors y Alicia García Navarro de D'Ors (Madrid: Alianza, 2002), 88.

Pedro Lasarte, *Lima satirizada (1598-1698): Mateo Rosas de Oquendo y Juan del Valle y Caviedes* (Lima: Pontificia Universidad Católica del Perú, 2006), 58–68.

Juan Rodríguez Freile, *El Carnero*, ed. Dario Achury Valenzuela (Caracas: Biblioteca Ayacucho, 1979), 36 [chap. 5].

Roberto González Echevarría, "Colonial Lyric," in González Echevarría and Pupo-Walker, *Cambridge History*, vol. 1, *Discovery to Modernism*, 219.

Paul Firbas, review of *Lima satirizada (1598-1698): Mateo Rosas de Oquendo y Juan del Valle y Caviedes* by Pedro Lasarte, in *Colonial Latin American Review* 19, no. 2 (August 2010): 362.

Pedro Lasarte, *Lima satirizada*, 21, 135, 143.

Chapter 8

Samuel Beckett, in *Anthology of Mexican Poetry*, ed. Octavio Paz, trans. Samuel Beckett (London: Thames and Hudson, 1968), 52.

Alan Trueblood, "Preface," in *A Sor Juana Anthology*, by Sor Juana Inés de la Cruz, trans. Alan Trueblood, foreword by Octavio Paz (Cambridge, MA: Harvard University Press, 1988), 11.

Jorge Luis Borges, "Homenaje a don Luis de Góngora" (1961), in *Textos recobrados 1956–1986* (Buenos Aires: Emecé Editores, 2003), 77.

Roberto González Echevarría, "Poetics and Modernity in Juan de Espinosa Medrano, Known as Lunarero," in *Celestina's Brood: Continuities of the Baroque in Spanish and Latin American Literature* (Durham, NC: Duke University Press, 1993), 161.

Rosa Perelmuter Pérez, *Noche intelectual: la oscuridad idiomática en el* Primero sueño (México: Universidad Nacional Autónoma de México, 1982).

Roberto González Echevarría, "Colonial Lyric," in González Echevarría and Pupo-Walker, *Cambridge History*, vol. 1, *Discovery to Modernism*, 226.

José Lezama Lima, "La curiosidad barroca," in *Confluencias: selección de ensayos*, ed. Abel E. Prieto (La Habana, 1988), 234.

D. A. Brading, *The First America: The Spanish Monarchy, Creole Patriots and the Liberal State, 1492–1867* (Cambridge: Cambridge University Press, 1991), 364–65.

Chapter 9

Emilio Carilla, *El Lazarillo de ciegos caminantes*, by Alonso Carrió de la Vandera ("Concolorcorvo"), ed. Emilio Carilla (Barcelona: Editorial Labor, 1973), 473n38.

Ruth Hill, *Hierarchy, Commerce, and Fraud in Bourbon Spanish America: A Postal Inspector's Exposé* (Nashville, TN: Vanderbilt University Press, 2005), 247.

Ruth Hill, "Churchmen, Statesmen, Smugglers *extraordinaires*: The Prodigious 4 P's from Lima," *Indiana Journal of Hispanic Literatures*, no. 8 (Spring 1996): 113–14.

Emilio Carilla, "Introducción," in *El Lazarillo de ciegos caminantes*, 52–60, 73.

Benjamin Keen, *The Aztec Image in Western Thought* (New Brunswick, NJ: Rutgers University Press, 1985), 180.

Jorge Cañizares Esguerra, "Spanish America in Eighteenth-Century European Travel Compilations: A New 'Art of Reading' and the Transition to Modernity," *Journal of Early Modern History* 2, no. 4 (1998): 330.

D. A. Brading, *The First America*, 585.

Andrés Bello, *Selected Writings of Andrés Bello*, trans. Frances M. López-Morillas, ed. Iván Jaksić (New York: Oxford University Press, 1997), 189, 191.

Aníbal González, "Literary Criticism in Spanish America," in González Echevarría and Pupo-Walker, *Cambridge History*, vol. 2, *The Twentieth Century*, 432.

Antonio Benítez Rojo, "The Nineteenth-Century Spanish American Novel," in González Echevarría and Pupo-Walker, *Cambridge History*, vol. 1, *Discovery to Modernism*, 418.

Andrés Bello, ed., *La Biblioteca americana, o Miscelánea de literatura, artes i ciencias*, 2 vols. (London: G. Marchant, 1823), 1:vii–viii.

Simón Bolívar, *El Libertador: Writings of Simón Bolívar*, trans. Frederick H. Fornoff, ed. David Bushnell (New York: Oxford University Press, 2003), 13.

Andrés Bello, *Selected Writings*, 8, 29.

Further reading

General

Adorno, Rolena. *The Polemics of Possession in Spanish American Narrative*. New Haven, CT: Yale University Press, 2007.

Brading, D. A. *The First America: The Spanish Monarchy, Creole Patriots, and the Liberal State, 1492–1867*. Cambridge: Cambridge University Press, 1991.

González Echevarría, Roberto. *Celestina's Brood: Continuities of the Baroque in Spanish and Latin American Literature*. Durham, NC: Duke University Press, 1993.

———. *Myth and Archive: A Theory of Latin American Narrative*. 1990. Durham, NC: Duke University Press, 1998.

González Echevarría, Roberto, and Enrique Pupo-Walker, eds. *The Cambridge History of Latin American Literature*. Vol. 1, *Discovery to Modernism*. Cambridge: Cambridge University Press, 1996.

Leonard, Irving A. *Books of the Brave: Being an Account of Books and Men in the Spanish Conquest and Settlement of the Sixteenth-Century New World*. 2nd ed. Edited and with a new critical introduction by Rolena Adorno. Berkeley: University of California Press, 1992.

Rodríguez Monegal, Emir, ed. With the assistance of Thomas Colchie. *The Borzoi Anthology of Latin American Literature from the Time of Columbus to the Twentieth Century*. Vol. 1. New York: Knopf, 1977.

Vicuña, Cecilia, and Ernesto Livon-Grosman, eds. *The Oxford Book of Latin American Poetry: A Bilingual Anthology*. New York: Oxford University Press, 2009.

Williamson, Edwin. *The Penguin History of Latin America*. Rev. ed. London: Penguin, 2009.

Introduction

Adorno, Rolena. "Cultures in Contact: Mesoamerica, the Andes and the European Written Tradition." In González Echevarría and Pupo-Walker, *Cambridge History of Latin American Literature*, 1:33–57, 3:437–52. Cambridge: Cambridge University Press, 1996.

——— . "Havana and Macondo: The Humanities in U.S. Latin American Studies, 1940–2000." In *The Humanities and the Dynamics of Inclusion since World War II*, edited and introduced by David A. Hollinger, 372–404. Cambridge, MA: American Academy of Arts and Sciences, 2006.

Chiapelli, Fredi, ed. *First Images of America*. 2 vols. Berkeley: University of California Press, 1976.

León-Portilla, Miguel, ed. *The Broken Spears: The Aztec Account of the Conquest of Mexico*. 1959.Translated from Nahuatl into Spanish by Ángel María Garibay. English translation by Lysander Kemp. Foreword by J. Jorge Klor de Alva. Boston: Beacon Press, 1992.

O'Gorman, Edmundo. *The Invention of America: An Inquiry into the Historical Nature of the New World and the Meaning of its History*. Bloomington: Indiana University Press, 1961.

Sahagún, Fr. Bernardino de. *Florentine Codex: Book 12: The Conquest of Mexico*. Edited and translated by Arthur J. O. Anderson and Charles E. Dibble. 2nd ed. Santa Fe: School of American Research and University of Utah, 1975.

——— . *General History of the Things of New Spain*. Edited and translated by Arthur J. O. Anderson and Charles E. Dibble. Santa Fe: School of American Research and University of Utah, 1982.

Salomon, Frank, and George L. Urioste, ed. and trans. *The Huarochirí Manuscript: A Testament of Ancient and Colonial Andean Religion*. Austin: University of Texas Press, 1991.

Tedlock, Dennis, ed. and trans. *Popol Vuh: The Mayan Book of the Dawn of Life*. New York: Simon and Schuster, 1985.

Chapter 1: First encounters, first doubts

Columbus, Christopher. *The Four Voyages of Columbus*. Edited and translated by Cecil Jane. New York: Dover, 1988.

Klor de Alva, J. Jorge, trans. "The Aztec-Spanish Dialogues (1524)," *Alcheringa* 4, no. 2 (1980): 52–193.

Pané, Fray Ramón. "The Relation of Fray Ramón Concerning the Antiquities of the Indians, which he, knowing their language, carefully compiled by order of the Admiral." In *The Life of the Admiral Christopher Columbus by His Son Ferdinand*, by Fernando Colón, edited and translated by Benjamin Keen, 153–69. New Brunswick, NJ: Rutgers University Press, 1992.

Restall, Matthew. *Seven Myths of the Spanish Conquest*. New York: Oxford University Press, 2003.

Todorov, Tzvetan. *The Conquest of America: The Question of the Other*. Translated by Richard Howard. New York: Harper and Row, 1984.

Chapter 2: Oviedo and Las Casas

Casas, Bartolomé de las. *History of the Indies*. Translated by Andrée Collard. New York: Harper and Row, 1971.

———. *A Selection of His Writings*. Translated by George Sanderlin. New York: Knopf, 1971.

———. *A Short Account of the Destruction of the Indies*. Translated by Nigel Griffin. Introduction by Anthony Pagden. New York: Penguin, 1992.

Fernández de Oviedo, Gonzalo. "Translations of passages from Fernández de Oviedo's *Historia general y natural de las Indias*." Translated by Nina M. Scott. In *Fernández de Oviedo's Chronicle of America: A New History of the New World*, by Kathleen A. Myers, 143–79. Austin: University of Texas Press, 2007.

Chapter 3: The polemics of possession

Casas, Bartolomé de las. *In Defense of the Indians*. Translated by Stafford Poole. Foreword by Martin E. Marty. DeKalb: Northern Illinois University Press, 1999. A translation of Las Casas's 1552–53 Latin *Apología*.

Pagden, Anthony. "Dispossessing the Barbarian: Rights and Property in Spanish America." In *Spanish Imperialism and the Political Imagination*, 13–36. New Haven, CT: Yale University Press, 1990.

Chapter 4: The conquest of Mexico

Adorno, Rolena. "The Narrative Invention of Gonzalo the Warrior." In *The Polemics of Possession in Spanish American Narrative*, 220–45. New Haven, CT: Yale University Press, 2007.

Chimalpahin Cuauhtlehuanitzin, Domingo Francisco de San Antón Muñón. *Chimalpahin's Conquest: A Nahua Historian's Rewriting*

of *Francisco López de Gómara's* La conquista de México. Edited
and translated by Susan Schroeder, Anne J. Cruz, Cristián
Roa-de-la-Carrera, and David E. Tavárez. Stanford, CA: Stanford
University Press, 2010.

Cortés, Hernán. *Letters from Mexico*. Translated by Anthony Pagden.
Introduction by J. H. Elliott. New Haven, CT: Yale University
Press, 1986.

Cypess, Sandra. "La Malinche as Palimpsest II." In *The History of the
Conquest of New Spain*, by Bernal Díaz del Castillo. Edited by
Davíd Carrasco, 418–38. Albuquerque: University of New Mexico
Press, 2008.

Díaz del Castillo, Bernal. *The History of the Conquest of New Spain*.
Edited by Davíd Carrasco. Albuquerque: University of New Mexico
Press, 2008.

Douglas, Eduardo de J. *In the Palace of Nezahualcoyotl: Painting
Manuscripts, Writing the Pre-Hispanic Past in Early Colonial
Texzcoco, Mexico*. Austin: University of Texas Press, 2010.

Powers, Karen Vieira. "Colonial Sexuality of Women, Men, and
Mestizaje." In Díaz del Castillo, *History of the Conquest of New
Spain*, 405–17.

Roa-de-la-Carrera, Cristián. *Histories of Infamy: Francisco López de
Gómara and the Ethics of Spanish Imperialism*. Boulder:
University Press of Colorado, 2005.

Chapter 5: A North American sojourn

Adorno, Rolena, and Patrick Charles Pautz. *Álvar Núñez Cabeza de
Vaca: His Account, His Life, and the Expedition of Pánfilo de
Narváez*. 3 vols. Lincoln: University of Nebraska Press, 1999.

Núñez Cabeza de Vaca, Álvar. *The Narrative of Cabeza de Vaca*. Edited,
translated, and with an introduction by Rolena Adorno and Patrick
Charles Pautz. Lincoln: University of Nebraska Press, 2003.

Chapter 6: Epic accomplishments

Acosta, José de. *Natural and Moral History of the Indies*. Translated by
Frances López-Morillas. Edited by Jane E. Mangan. Introduction
by Walter Mignolo. Durham, NC: Duke University Press, 2002.

Vega, El Inca Garcilaso de la. *Royal Commentaries of the Incas*.
Translated by Harold V. Livermore. Foreword by Arnold J. Toynbee.
Austin: University of Texas Press, 1966.

Chapter 7: Urban Baroque

Adorno, Rolena. *Guaman Poma: Writing and Resistance in Colonial Peru*. 2nd ed., with a new introduction. Austin: University of Texas Press, 2000.

Charles, John. *Allies at Odds: The Andean Church and Its Indigenous Agents, 1583–1671*. Albuquerque: University of New Mexico Press, 2010.

González Echevarría, Roberto. "Colonial Lyric." In González Echevarría and Pupo-Walker, *Cambridge History of Latin American Literature*, 1:191–230. Cambridge: Cambridge University Press, 1996.

Guaman Poma de Ayala, Felipe. *The First New Chronicle and Good Government*. Abridged. Selected, translated, and annotated by David Frye. Indianapolis, IN: Hackett, 2006.

———. *The First New Chronicle and Good Government: On the History of the World and the Incas up to 1615*. Edited and translated by Roland Hamilton. Austin: University of Texas Press, 2009.

———. *Nueva corónica y buen gobierno*. Edited by John V. Murra and Rolena Adorno, Quechua translations by Jorge L. Urioste. 3 vols. México: Siglo XXI Editores, 1980. (http://www.kb.dk/permalink/2006/poma/info/en/frontpage.htm)

Rodríguez Freile, Juan. *The Conquest of New Granada*. Translated by William C. Atkinson. London: Folio Society, 1961.

Yannakakis, Yanna. *The Art of Being In-Between: Native Intermediaries, Indian Identity, and Local Rule in Colonial Oaxaca*. Durham, NC: Duke University Press, 2008.

Chapter 8: Baroque plenitude

Díaz, Mónica. *Indigenous Writings from the Convent: Negotiating Ethnic Autonomy in Colonial Mexico*. Tucson: University of Arizona Press, 2010.

Góngora, Luis de. *The Solitudes of Luis de Góngora*. Translated by Gilbert F. Cunningham. Preface by A. A. Parker. Introduction by Elias L. Rivers. Baltimore: Johns Hopkins University Press, 1968.

González Echevarría, Roberto. "Poetics and Modernity in Juan de Espinosa Medrano, Known as Lunarejo." In *Celestina's Brood*, 149–69.

Juana Inés de la Cruz, Sor. *The Answer/La Respuesta, Including a Selection of Poems*. Edited and translated by Electa Arenal and Amanda Powell. New York: Feminist Press, 1994.

————. *A Sor Juana Anthology*. Translated by Alan S. Trueblood. Foreword by Octavio Paz. Cambridge, MA: Harvard University Press, 1988.

————. *Sor Juana Inés de la Cruz: Poems*. Translated by Margaret Sayers Peden. Binghamton, NY: Bilingual Press, 1985.

————. *A Woman of Genius: The Intellectual Autobiography of Sor Juana Inés de la Cruz*. Translated and with an introduction by Margaret Sayers Peden. Salisbury, CT: Lime Rock Press, 1982.

Leonard, Irving A. *Baroque Times in Old Mexico*. 1959. Ann Arbor: University of Michigan Press, 1993.

Myers, Kathleen Ann. *Neither Saints nor Sinners: Writing the Lives of Women in Spanish America*. New York: Oxford University Press, 2003.

Myers, Kathleen Ann, and Amando Powell, eds. *A Wild Country Out in the Garden: The Spiritual Journals of a Colonial Mexican Nun*. Bloomington: Indiana University Press, 1999.

Paz, Octavio, ed. *Anthology of Mexican Poetry*. Translated by Samuel Beckett. Preface by C. M. Bowra. London: Thames and Hudson, 1958.

————. *Sor Juana, or the Traps of Faith*. Translated by Margaret Sayers Peden. Cambridge, MA: Harvard University Press, 1988.

Chapter 9: On to independence

Arenas, Reinaldo. *The Ill-Fated Peregrinations of Fray Servando*. Translated by Andrew Hurley. New York: Penguin, 1987.

Bello, Andrés. *Selected Writings of Andrés Bello*. Translated by Frances M. López-Morillas. Edited and with an introduction and notes by Iván Jaksić. New York: Oxford University Press, 1997.

Bolívar, Simón. *El Libertador: Writings of Simón Bolívar*. Translated by Frederick H. Fornoff. Edited by David Bushnell. New York: Oxford University Press, 2003.

Concolorcorvo (Carrió de la Vandera, Alonso). *El Lazarillo: A Guide for Inexperienced Travelers between Buenos Aires and Lima, 1773*. Translated by Walter D. Kline. Bloomington: Indiana University Press, 1965.

Hill, Ruth. *Hierarchy, Commerce, and Fraud in Bourbon Spanish America: A Postal Inspector's Exposé*. Nashville, TN: Vanderbilt University Press, 2005.

Mier, Fray Servando Teresa de. *The Memoirs of Fray Servando Teresa de Mier*. Edited and with an introduction by Susana Rotker. Translated by Helen Lane. New York: Oxford University Press, 1998.

Index

Index